P9-BYG-223

HANDY DAD

IN THE GREAT OUTDOORS

BY TODD DAVIS   PHOTOGRAPHS BY JARED CRUCE AND TODD DAVIS
ILLUSTRATIONS BY NIK SCHULZ

MORE THAN 30 SUPER-COOL PROJECTS AND ACTIVITIES FOR DADS AND KIDS

CHRONICLE BOOKS
SAN FRANCISCO

Text copyright © 2012 by Todd Davis.

Photographs copyright © 2012 by Jared Cruce and Todd Davis.

Illustrations copyright © 2012 by Nik Schulz.

All rights reserved. No part of this book may be reproduced in any form without written permission from the publisher.

Library of Congress Cataloging-in-Publication Data:

Davis, Todd, 1972–

    Handy dad in the great outdoors : more than 30 super-cool projects and activities for dads and kids / Todd Davis.

      p. cm.

    ISBN 978-1-4521-0213-9

    1. Camping. 2. Outdoor recreation. 3. Family recreation. I. Title.

GV191.7.D38 2011

796.54—dc23

                              2011022563

Manufactured in China

Designed by Cody Haltom, Steph Davlantes, & Blake Suárez

As with any project, it is important to follow all instructions carefully; failure to do so could result in injury. Every effort has been made to present the information in this book in a clear, complete, and accurate manner; however, not every situation can be anticipated and there is no substitute for your own common sense. Check product labels to make sure that the materials you use are safe and nontoxic. Nontoxic is a description given to any substance that does not give off dangerous fumes or contain harmful ingredients (such as chemicals or poisons) in amounts that could endanger a person's health. Be careful when handling dangerous objects. The authors and Chronicle Books disclaim any and all liability resulting from injuries or damage caused during the production or use of the crafts discussed in this book.

Android is a registered trademark of Google Inc. BioBag is a registered trademark of PolarGruppen AS Corp. Bag-to Nature is a registered trademark of Indaco Manufacturing Ltd. Coghlan's is a registered trademark of Coghlan's Ltd. Crocs is a registered trademark of Crocs Inc. Dr. Bronner's is a registered trademark of All-One-God-Faith Inc. Feline Pine is a registered trademark of PlanetWise Products Inc. Frisbee is a registered trademark of Wham-O Inc. Fruit Roll-Ups is a registered trademark of General Mills Inc. Gamma Seal is a registered trademark of Gamma Plastics Co. Gold Guzzler and Super Sluice are registered trademarks of Garrett Electronics Inc. Google Maps and Google Earth are registered trademarks of Google Inc. Groundspeak is a registered trademark of Grounded Inc. Hello Kitty is a registered trademark of Sanrio Company, Ltd. Hershey's Milk Chocolate and Reese's Pieces are registered trademarks of Hershey Chocolate & Confectionery Corp. iPad is a registered trademark of Apple Inc. Kevlar and Teflon are registered trademarks of E. I. du Pont de Nemours and Co. Knox is a registered trademark of NBTY Inc. Leatherman is a registered trademark of Leatherman Tool Group Inc. Luhr-Jensen Super Duper is a registered trademark of Rapala VMC Oyj Joint Stock Co. Maglite is a registered trademark of Mag Instrument Inc. Mentos is a registered trademark of Perfetti Van Melle Benelux B.V. Ltd. Micropur is a registered trademark of Katadyn Produkte Ag Corp. Neosporin is a registered trademark of Johnson & Johnson Corp. Oreo is a registered trademark of Kraft Foods Global Brands LLC. Otter Pop is a registered trademark of Jel Sert Co. Popsicle is a registered trademark of Lipton Investments Inc. Scotch Tape is a registered trademark of Minnesota Mining and Manufacturing Co. Styrofoam is a registered trademark of Dow Chemical Co. Silva is a registered trademark of Johnson Worldwide Associates Inc. Suunto is a registered trademark of Suunto Oy Corp. Brunton is a registered trademark of Fenix Outdoor AB. Therm-a-Rest is a registered trademark of Cascade Designs Inc. Velcro is a registered trademark of Velcro Industries B.V. Ltd. Tron is a registered trademark of Disney Enterprises. X-ACTO is a registered trademark of Elmer's Products Inc. Ziploc is a registered trademark of S. C. Johnson Home Storage Inc.

10 9 8 7 6 5 4 3 2 1

Chronicle Books LLC

680 Second Street

San Francisco, California 94107

www.chroniclebooks.com

MIX
Paper from responsible sources
FSC
www.fsc.org   FSC® C104723

CONTENTS

INTRODUCTION

My parents spoiled me—but not with stuff. They didn't cater to my every whim and whine. I didn't have all the latest and greatest toys. I made good use of a hand-me-down bicycle, soccer ball, and football. I wasn't rewarded with an exorbitant allowance for grudgingly completing simple chores.

Instead, my parents spoiled me with outdoor adventures and experiences. But until I was an adult, I took it for granted. When I was a kid, I just assumed everyone's parents took them waterskiing, snow skiing, fishing, hunting, and camping or backpacking each weekend. We were on outdoor-adventure expeditions so often that I just thought it was normal.

These weekly sojourns were always fun, but not always easy. My parents would never reach the destination and simply throw the car doors open and let us kids just run amok. From a very young age, no matter the activity, self-reliance was the primary lesson. We were expected to be able to pack everything we would need for the whole trip. Forgetting a sleeping bag meant a cold night or two, to be sure, but you were unlikely to forget again. We were taught how to use the gear properly. Forgetting or feigning ignorance wouldn't get it set up for you, but my parents were always ready to show you again. We were also taught to respect our safety, gear, and environment. Failure to do so meant staying home the following weekend with a babysitter.

We were exposed to new things constantly, learned new things constantly, and shared things constantly. I truly believe these outdoor adventures made us the close-knit family we are.

Today I find myself with a family of my own. My beautiful wife has blessed me with two young sons. These little rascals have quickly evolved from crawling up the stairs to BASE jumping off the couch. I look forward to the day when my boys are old enough to go on adventures with me. I have a great deal to share with them that I've picked up over the years. And I've included it all here in this book, from basic survival skills to humorous pranks to pull on big or little brothers (never Dad, but Mom might be OK), along with outdoor activities and projects to do together. There are a range of projects from easy (Weekend Warrior) and moderate (Car Camper) to challenging (Backwoodsman).

Easy   Moderate   Challenging

I hope this book will inspire you to go outside—whether that means the backcountry or your backyard—and explore and experiment. Anyone can light a fire with a match in seconds, but take two sticks, two hours, and two young sons. Good times.

CHOOSE THE BEST CAMPSITE

Picking the right location to pitch your tent can make the difference between a great camping trip and a dud. How can you find a spot that will make for a memorable time instead of a miserable one? Read on.

DIFFICULTY LEVEL:
Weekend Warrior

MATERIALS:

Your noggin

Maps

Online resources

INSTRUCTIONS:

1 Start your campsite-scouting from home. The National Park Service (nps.gov), the Bureau of Land Management (blm.gov), and your own state parks website are great places to start. If you live in or are heading to the West, look at www.sunset.com. Other regional or city magazines may also offer insights for local trips. Or pull out your favorite guidebook or map. *National Geographic* offers an *Adventure* edition road atlas that not only displays campgrounds prominently but also features overviews of all of the national parks. Benchmark Maps publishes detailed and informative state atlases that are also worth a look. For a more personal take on traveling, research blogs. And ask your friends where they've gone lately.

2 Once you have a general area in mind, have a look at it on Google Maps or Google Earth. Look for features of interest such as high alpine lakes and streams and dramatic elevation changes. Consult the NPS or BLM, if applicable, to see which specific areas are open for camping. If reservations are required, reserve early. Popular spots can fill up weeks or even months in advance.

3 Once you've isolated the area you're interested in, buy a good-quality topographic map (USGS, for example). What are the notable features of your chosen area? What must you look out for?

4 When you're out in the field, with your map in hand, start looking for the following:

A freshwater source

A flat site that provides protection from the sun, wind, and rain.

A downed tree or other source of firewood (Check local regulations regarding wood gathering before you go.)

An interesting feature that will make your trip more memorable, e.g., a large lakeside boulder or fallen tree from which to dive or fish, a grassy meadow, or a great trail or view.

5 If you're car camping at a campground, pick a spot away from the heavily traveled parts of the camp. It's no fun to constantly have car headlights shining through your camp. Keep water sources in mind. Being relatively close to one means a shorter distance to lug water containers. It's a good idea to be close enough to the toilets so that you can see them at night, but not so close that you can smell them. Take note of which way the wind blows.

6 Once you've considered all your options, pick the site that feels right. Find a flat spot to pitch your tent. Think about where the sun will rise in the morning. If it's cold out, pitch in a sunny spot. If it's warm out, a tent may quickly get uncomfortably hot in direct sun.

7 Are you all settled in? Good. Now find two trees from which to hang your hammock and reap the benefits of your well-executed plan!

SET UP A TENT

There are stunning, soul-stirring views all over the world. What's the best way to experience them? Well, you could stay in a fancy lodge. But for the same amount you might spend on a single night in a lodge, you can kit out your own vacation hideaway, a portable palace that you can take deep into the forest, to the edge of a burbling stream, or to the top of a mountain. Yes, sir, all you need is a good tent.

DIFFICULTY LEVEL:
Weekend Warrior

MATERIALS:

3-person tent

Any tent you purchase will likely come with most of the following items:

- Tent bag
- Tent poles and bag
- Rain fly
- Tent stakes and bag
- Guy lines with tensioners (bring 4 extra guy lines if it's going to be windy)
- Tent-pole repair tube

Footprint for tent, if not included. (This is optional, but highly recommended for additional protection from punctures and abrasion. If you can't find a footprint for your tent, a tarp will work as well.)

Therm-a-Rest or other camping pad

2-inch foam pad (if you're car camping and like things extra cushy)

Bedding (sleeping bag if you're backpacking, or sheets and pillows if you're car camping in style)

TOOLS:

Hammer, camp axe, or rock

INSTRUCTIONS:

NOTE: These directions apply broadly to any tent with an external pole structure.

1 See "Choose the Best Campsite," page 8, to find a majestic 10-by-10-foot campsite free of rocks, roots, and debris, but close to a water source.

2 Get out your tent's footprint and lay it on the ground, with the coated side up. If it's windy, stake the footprint down. Be aware of which way your rain fly opens and orient the footprint so that you'll be facing the view. See image **a**.

3 Lay your tent on top of the footprint so that the short sides of the tent and the footprint match. See image **b**.

4 Get out your tent poles and follow the instructions specific to your tent for setting them up. Usually the poles are color-coded to the tabs they match. If your tent employs a pole-and-sleeve system, thread the poles through the sleeves, then insert them into the tabs on the footprint and tent. If your tent uses a pole-and-hook system, insert the ends of the poles into the tabs on the footprint, then hook the tent to the poles. If the tabs have two sets of grommets, use the outer set. See images **c** and **d**.

5 Alright—your tent should be up. At this point, pick it up and double-check that there's no debris under it. How's the view? Move the tent to tune the view to your liking. See image **e**.

6 Now grab the rain fly and throw it over the tent, making sure to align the colored tabs. See image **f**. Lining these tabs up will keep the window of the fly lined up with the window on the tent. Your rain fly will most likely have some Velcro fasteners, which should be attached around the tent poles. Do that, then wrap the fabric tabs under the tabs of the tent and footprint, and insert the ends of the poles through the grommets. See image **g**.

7 OK—your tent is done. It's time to stake it down. Place a tent stake through each loop at the ends of the tabs and, using your hammer, the blunt end of your camp axe, or even a rock, drive the stakes into the ground. The hooks should face outward. See image **h**.

8 Stake down the vestibule flaps, too. Now tighten all of the buckles on the fabric tabs attached to the rain fly. See image **i**.

9 If it's windy, tie the free end of each guy line to a guy-out point on the rain fly. (Those are the little fabric loops on the surface of the fly.) Pull a loop out of the guy-line tensioner, stake the line down through that loop, then slide the tensioner toward the tent to make the line taught.

10 Unzip the doors of your mini-mansion and toss in your Therm-a-Rest. If you're car camping and would like to make your digs truly luxurious, pack a two-inch foam mattress, pillows, sheets, and an old-school sleeping bag to unzip for use as a comforter. If it weren't for the rip-stop nylon and zippers, you'd swear you were sleeping in the finest lodge. See image **j**.

BUILD THE PERFECT FIRE

A roaring fire is the heart of any campsite—whether you use it for cooking, signaling, keeping warm, or just plain old enjoying. Build it well and you're in for a good night. Build it poorly and it will be a source of frustration. Here, I'll show you how to build a basic fire, plus a couple of useful variations to suit different situations.

DIFFICULTY LEVEL:
Car Camper

Regardless of which type of fire you'll be building, start by finding a fire pit or other clear, safe area. If you need to create an area yourself, clear a 10-foot-diameter circle down to bare earth and build your fire in the middle of it. All fires start from the same three-tiered combination of tinder, kindling, and medium-size sticks of firewood. Let's gather those now.

MATERIALS:

10 to 16 pieces straight, dry firewood, roughly 12 by 2 inches

8 to 12 straight, dry, roughly 6-by-1-inch twigs for kindling

6-inch-wide fire nest made of small twigs, pine needles, leaves, etc., for tinder

Lighter, matches, or other fire-starting materials (See Start a Fire Without a Match on page 50 for further info.)

TOOLS:

Axe or thick branch to use as a hammer

Shovel

Bucket

INSTRUCTIONS:

PYRE OR STACKED FIRE

This is a great low-maintenance fire. Once it's burning, it will stay lit for hours.

1 Build a stepped pyramid out of the logs. Start by laying the two largest logs in the fire pit parallel with each other and about 2 feet apart.

2 . Stack the next two biggest logs centered perpendicularly across the first two and about 18 inches apart. See image **a**.

3 Continue stacking in this fashion using smaller logs for each step until your pyramid is four or five layers high.

4 Make two additional layers out of the smallest logs. Instead of using only two logs per layer, however, use several. These will be the platform layers. See image **b**.

5 On top of this platform, build a tepee fire as described on page 16. Instead of pounding the tinder and kindling into the ground, however, brace them against the surrounding logs.

6 The fire will burn through the pyramid from the top down with little maintenance needed. Light and enjoy.

INSTRUCTIONS:

TEPEE FIRE

1 Gather your pine needles and leaves (or scraps of paper) into a loose nest shape and place them in the center of the pit.

2 Form a tepee around the fire nest with the tinder sticks. Be sure to press the ends of the tinder into the ground so they're stable. See image **c**.

3 Now form a tepee over the tinder with the kindling. Start by arranging two pieces opposite each other so they form a triangle over the tinder. With your axe or a thick branch, hit the tops of both pieces simultaneously and pound them into the ground.

4 Do the same thing with two other pieces of kindling so that the four pieces form a pyramid with a square base.

5 Lay the rest of the kindling against this frame to form a solid-walled tepee. Leave an opening facing the wind. See image **d**.

6 Light the nest in two places and let the fire burn 2 to 3 minutes before adding larger pieces of wood to the outside of the tepee. See images **e** and **f**.

7 Enjoy your roaring fire. Gather with friends and tell tall tales.

c

d

e

f

LEAN-TO FIRE

Use this structure if you're building a fire in heavy winds or rain. It will provide a shelter that allows the flames to build.

MATERIALS

One 1- to 3-inch-wide Y-shaped branch

1 straight, dry branch, roughly 3 feet long by 2 inches wide

Fourteen to eighteen 2-inch-wide branches, broken into two sets with incremental lengths from 6 to 18 inches

Plus all the general fire materials (see page 15)

TOOLS

Camp shovel

INSTRUCTIONS

1 Find a spot downwind from the center of the fire pit and dig a hole deep enough to support the end of your Y branch.

2 Put the end of the branch in the hole so that a line across the top of the Y is perpendicular to a line toward the center of the fire pit. Pack in the hole to secure the branch.

3 Place one end of the 3-foot branch in the crook of the Y and the other across the center of the fire pit (it will be pointing in the direction of the wind). This branch will be the backbone of your lean-to. See image **g**.

4 Placing the branches as close together as possible, build the sides of the lean-to with the two sets of 2-inch-wide branches. Start with the longest branches closest to the Y and end with the shortest where the backbone touches the ground. See image **h**.

5 Build a tepee fire inside the lean-to. Instead of setting the kindling with your hammer, use a stick to dig three or four indentations in the bottom of the fire pit and use them to brace the kindling. Light the nest in two different locations. Continue adding fuel as the fire builds. The wind will feed it but won't be able to blow the fire out.

A Note on Safety

When you're ready to leave camp, there's only one way to ensure that your fire is out, and stomping it down and covering it with dirt isn't it. To properly and safely put out your fire, pour buckets of water on to the ashes and stir them with a shovel until there's nothing left but smoke-free mud. Even a fire that hasn't burned for a few hours will still throw a surprising amount of ash and smoke into the air when the first bucket of water hits it, so stand back for the first volley.

CAMPFIRE COOKING:
S'MORES, BANANA BOATS, AND DOGS!

Camping is great, isn't it? Sleeping under the stars, sitting around the campfire, waking up to birds singing, swimming, and hiking are all pretty thrilling. And what makes it even better? The menu! Hot dogs, s'mores, and banana boats make for delicious campfire fare!

DIFFICULTY LEVEL:
Weekend Warrior

MATERIALS:

Several 3- to 4-foot-long wooden sticks or unpainted wire coat hangers

1 roll aluminum foil

Campfire with lots of hot coals

TOOLS:

Pocketknife or pliers

Spoons

Wire cutters

INSTRUCTIONS TO MAKE A ROASTING STICK:

1 You can make your cooking tools out of wire coat hangers or wooden sticks. I prefer sticks because they're easy to find and easier to control. Of course, if you goof up and cook too close to the fire, you'll end up making a torch instead of dinner. Coat hangers won't burn, but they're a bit wobbly. Take your pick.

2 If you're using sticks, find ones at least ½ inch wide at the base. Clean off all the extraneous branches and sharpen the ends to a point with your pocketknife. If you can find sticks with forked branches at the ends, so much the better.

3 If you're using coat hangers, clip both sides of the wire below the hook and straighten them out.

4 Put on your chef's hat.

INSTRUCTIONS:

S'MORES

Serves up to six people

These have been a campfire classic for almost as long as there have been campfires. This version is a twist on the classic.

MATERIALS

One 14-ounce box plain or cinnamon graham crackers

3 to 6 milk chocolate bars (plan on 1.5 ounces per person)

1 jar creamy peanut butter

One 10-ounce bag large marshmallows

INSTRUCTIONS

1 Break the graham cracker in half and cover it with a slab of chocolate. See image **a**.

2 Spread peanut butter over the other half. See image **b**.

3 Push the stick almost, but not all the way, through the marshmallow and slowly rotate it just above the flames until it's golden brown. This will take about a minute. See image **c**.

4 Put the marshmallow between the chocolate and the peanut butter side of the other graham cracker. Squeeze the whole thing and pull the marshmallow off the stick. See image **d**.

5 Look around, see who's suffering the most from highly debilitating "Needa s'morkum" syndrome, and quickly hand them a s'more.

6 Make one for yourself, too. Rest assured that you'll be hounded for more s'mores until your supplies are toasted (literally).

HOT DOGS

MATERIALS

1 or 2 hot dogs per person

Buns

Your favorite condiments

INSTRUCTIONS

1 Hot dogs are easy. Pierce a hot dog on your roasting stick. Rotate it about a foot above the coals for 5 minutes. It's done.

2 If you're at a campsite with a fire ring and a grate, give the buns a little toast.

3 Assemble and enjoy!

BANANA BOATS

Serves six.

MATERIALS

Aluminum foil

6 bananas

One 10-ounce bag mini marshmallows

One 12-ounce bag chocolate chips or Reese's Pieces

One 2.5-ounce bag minced almonds, walnuts, or pecans

INSTRUCTIONS

1 Tear off a 12-inch piece of aluminum foil and fold it in half.

2 Peel one strip of the banana skin open along the inside part of its curve and keep the peel attached.

3 Slice the banana lengthwise down the middle and open it like a baked potato. See image **e**.

4 Place the banana onto the foil with the open side up.

5 Pour about 20 mini marshmallows and 30 chocolate chips or Reese's Pieces into the banana. See image **f**.

6 Sprinkle about a tablespoon of nuts on top of the marshmallows and chocolate. See image **g**.

7 Fold the peel back down over the ingredients and smash them together a bit. See image **h**.

8 Seal the banana completely in the foil. See image **i**.

9 Repeat process with the other five bananas and place them all in the coals of the fire. See image **j**.

10 Let them sit for 5 minutes, and then rotate them.

11 Leave them in the fire for 3 more minutes, pull them out, and let them cool a bit.

12 Open the foil and serve each one with a spoon. Dig in!

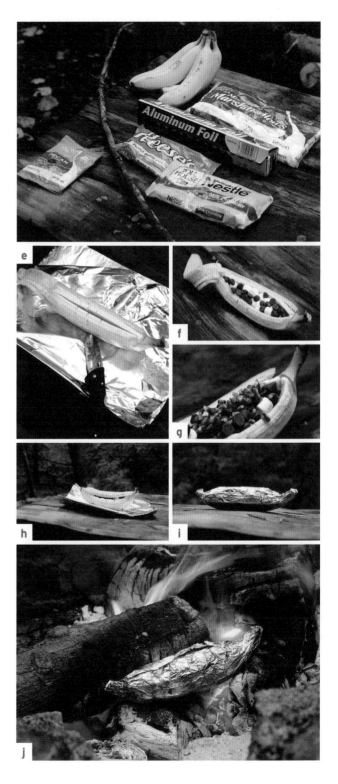

PROTECT BEARS FROM YOUR FOOD

Bears are amazing—from a distance. But if they get the idea that your campsite is the backwoods equivalent of a taco truck, things can get ugly pretty fast. Whatever you do, don't hide food in your tent for "safekeeping" before you tuck in for the night. You might as well wrap yourself in bacon and stand out in the woods blowing a bear whistle. Even the clothes you cook meat or fish in can attract bears. Once bears get a taste for human food, they come back for more, quickly become "problem bears," and meet a quick end. A sign I once saw at a campsite put it this way: "A fed bear is a dead bear." So do the bears (and yourself) a favor and protect them from your tasty treats.

DIFFICULTY LEVEL:
Weekend Warrior

MATERIALS:

Bear canister, tested and approved by the National Park Service (Check the National Park Service website, http://www.nps.gov, for a list of canisters approved for the park you plan to visit.)

50 feet parachute cord

Carabiner

Tall tree

Note: In many states including Alaska, California, and Washington, a bear canister is required for wilderness camping.

Another option is a Kevlar bag. But these offer less protection. I stand by the old-school method I describe here: a bear can and a tall tree.

INSTRUCTIONS:

1 Place all of your food in the bear canister. Don't forget to throw in ointments, lotions, toothpaste, powders, deodorants, sunscreen, bug sprays, and any utensils you cooked with. Bears have a nose for curious smells and will come to investigate.

2 Fold about 10 inches of one end of the cord back on itself to form a bight. Tie that bight into a knot to form a loop. See image **a**.

3 Wrap the knotted end of the para cord once around the bear canister. At the point where the knotted loop meets up with the standing part of the cord, thread a bight back through the loop. See image **b**.

4 Pull this bight so that you have plenty of slack, and fold it over the top of the bear canister. Ensure that the cord doesn't travel back on itself after going through the loop, but continues around the can. This will help it grip better. Pull the standing part of the cord tight to cinch the wraps down. See **Tying the Bear Vault** illustration.

5 At the other end of the cord, make another knotted loop on a bight (just like in Step 2) and snap your carabiner through the loop. See image **c**.

6 Look for a tree at least 200 feet downwind of your campsite. You're looking for one with a branch between 2 and 4 inches in diameter and about 15 to 20 feet off the ground. The idea here is to find a branch that's far enough off the ground that a bear, standing on its hind legs, could not reach your food, and that's also thin enough to discourage a bear cub from climbing the tree and walking out on the branch. If you're above the tree line, place a large rock on the bear can. The bear may be curious but he won't get the can open even if he knocks the rock off. You'll probably have to go looking for your canister in the morning, though.

7 OK—now we're going to throw the carabiner end of the line over the branch. Aim for a spot at least 10 feet away from the trunk. Before you swing that carabiner though, have the rest of the cord flaked neatly out on the ground so it doesn't tangle and stop the carabiner in mid flight. It could wrap around the branch and get stuck, a headache you don't need.

8 Did it make it over the branch? If it's hanging over the other side but not touching the ground, give the cord a whip to send a wave through the line. This will momentarily release the friction on the cord and allow the carabiner to fall to the ground. See image **d**.

9 Now lift the bear vault over your head with one hand (preferably the stronger one). With your other hand, pull the slack out of the line so that the can remains aloft.

10 Keep the cord tight and pull the can the rest of the way up. It should be about 15 feet off of the ground.

11 Secure the cord to the tree by wrapping the carabiner end around the trunk, or a lower branch, and then clipping the carabiner back to the cord itself. See image **e**.

12 Now you can go back to camp and rest soundly, knowing that you're not sleeping in a bear pantry. And you can pat yourself on the back for helping keep bears safe from people food. See image **f**.

Fold bight over
top of the canister.

Tying the Bear Vault

BUILD A BIODEGRADABLE LATRINE

When nature calls, you don't have to answer in a smelly pit toilet or trudge half a mile from camp with a shovel in hand. All you need is this ecologically (and literally) green bucket. That, and a little privacy, of course.

DIFFICULTY LEVEL:
Weekend Warrior

MATERIALS:

1-gallon bulk-storage container with a wide mouth

2 rolls of toilet paper (Look for rolls made with 100 percent recycled fiber, 80 percent post-consumer, and whitened without elemental chlorine.*)

1-gallon Ziploc bag

Green 12-inch Gamma Seal screw-on lid

Green 5-gallon bucket

13-gallon trash bags, either BioBag or Bag to Nature brand (BioBags are made from corn. Heat from urine may cause them to leak, so use three or four. Bag to Nature trash bags are made from 100 percent compostable, organic biopolymers. They're much stronger, but double up just in case.)

Ten 3-inch cable ties

3 feet ½-inch (inside diameter) foam pipe insulation

4-pound bag kitty litter (I prefer the Feline Pine brand.)

*These supplies will serve two people on a weekend trip. Bring more or fewer supplies, depending on your needs.

No forest of any kind should be used to make toilet paper. —Old proverb

INSTRUCTIONS:

1 Fill your 1-gallon bulk-storage container with Feline Pine and seal the lid. See image **a**.

2 Place two rolls of toilet paper in the Ziploc bag to keep them clean and dry. Toss the 10 cable ties in there, too.

3 Snap the Gamma Seal lid in place on the bucket—it takes firm pressure, all the way around—and remove the screw-down interior lid.

4 Place the rest of your supplies in the bucket and screw the lid back in place. See image **b**. You're now ready for travel!

5 Choose a comfortable spot protected from the sun and wind. A little group of trees will do the job. Maybe you can even find a spot with a view. For the benefit of your fellow campers, head downwind about 200 feet.

6 Did you find a spot? Great—take out your supplies and line the inside of the bucket with two to four trash bags, depending on the brand you chose.

7 Pour enough Feline Pine into the bucket to cover the bottom. A quarter of your container should do it. See image **c**.

8 Attach the pipe insulation to the rim of the bucket. This will give you a comfy seat and hold the bag in place. Keep the toilet paper in reach! See image **d**.

9 Did you bring this book with you? Fantastic—you've got some reading material! Ah . . . it sure beats sitting in a smelly old outhouse, doesn't it?

10 Throw the toilet paper you used into the bucket and sprinkle in enough Feline Pine to cover your waste.

11 Rest the screw-in portion of the Gamma Seal lid on the pipe insulation and weigh it down with a rock.

12 When it's time to go home, remove the lid, gather the open end of the bags together, and twist them closed as far down as possible. Tie the bag off twice with cable ties (just to be sure) and leave the whole thing in the bucket.

13 Screw the Gamma Seal lid in place. You'll have to find another location for the rest of your supplies for the ride home.

14 Pick a spot in your car that will keep the bucket stationary and upright. Drive to the nearest legal place to throw away your waste.

15 When you get home, wash the entire bucket and pipe insulation with biodegradable soap.

16 Put all of your supplies back in the bucket and seal it for the next use. Try to use the trash bags within a year though. They tend to degrade over time.

17 Congratulate yourself on having discovered a way to take nature's call out of the dank outhouse dungeon and into the great outdoors.

BUILD A SOLAR SHOWER

Yeah, nothing beats roughing it, except for—maybe—the stink. Days of whacking through bushes, trekking through forests, and forging up peaks are all well and good, but what to do when you come back to camp so odiferous that not even your dog wants to share your tent? When you need a little help leaving the wilderness behind, nothing beats a clean, hot, solar-powered shower, except for—maybe—getting dirty again.

DIFFICULTY LEVEL:
Car Camper

MATERIALS:

Black 5-gallon bucket (A black bucket will do the best job of absorbing the sun's rays.)

Black 12-inch Gamma Seal screw-on lid

Two ¾-inch rubber washers

¾-by-1½-inch stainless steel washer

Teflon tape

¾-inch PVC close riser (double-threaded)

½-inch poly elbow

¾-inch brass nut

3-foot piece ½-inch clear poly tubing (second piece optional*)

½-inch poly adapter (second adapter optional*)

½-inch King ball valve

TOOLS:

Pencil

Tape measure

Drill with ¾-inch spade bit

Pocket/utility knife

Vise grips

Crescent wrench

*An additional poly adapter and length of tubing can be added to the ball valve to extend the reach of your shower for washing dishes, boots, or other low-to-the-ground items, like kids.

INSTRUCTIONS:

1 Make a mark on the bucket that's 1¾ inches from the bottom and midway between the two handle supports. If you can't find your tape measure, lay the rubber washer down next to the bucket, set your stainless-steel washer on top of it, and mark the center of the hole. See image **a**.

2 Using the ¾-inch spade bit, slowly drill a hole through your mark.

3 Apply Teflon tape to both the PVC riser and the poly tube adapter. Looking at the threaded end of each part, apply the tape in a clockwise direction to keep the tail end of the tape from getting scrunched up as you screw the parts together. See image **b**.

4 Screw the PVC riser into the ½-inch poly elbow as far as possible. Use the vise grips if you need to, but don't tighten the riser so much that you damage the plastic threads. To see how all the parts will come together, see **Connection to Bucket** illustration and image **c**.

5 Place the ¾-inch rubber washer and the stainless-steel washer over the hole on the outside of the bucket. The rubber washer should be between the bucket and the steel washer. Make sure they're both perfectly aligned over the hole. See image **d**.

6 Insert the threaded end of the poly elbow through the washers and screw it into the bucket. Keep going until enough threads show to support the other rubber washer and the ¾-inch brass nut.

7 If the Teflon tape on the threads has come off, just add more. Looking good? OK—add the rubber washer and screw on the brass nut on the inside of the bucket. Use the crescent wrench to make sure it's nice and tight. See image **e**.

8 Attach the ½-inch poly tubing onto the poly elbow, making sure it covers at least three of the ridged rings. If the tube is difficult to fit, heat the end of it a bit to make it more pliable. See image **f**.

9 Now let's work on the valve. Apply Teflon tape to the adapter (clockwise when looking at the threaded end, same as before), and screw it into the valve. Use the crescent wrench to get a tight fit. See image **g**.

10 Insert the adapter end of the valve into the open end of the poly tubing as far as it will go (covering at least three rings) and check to make sure that the valve is closed. Again, heat the tubing if it's a difficult fit. See image **h**.

11 Put the Gamma Seal lid onto the top of the bucket and press down firmly, all the way around the rim, to seal it. Now unscrew the center lid. See image **i**.

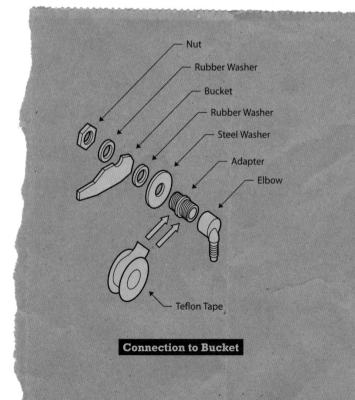

Nut
Rubber Washer
Bucket
Rubber Washer
Steel Washer
Adapter
Elbow
Teflon Tape

Connection to Bucket

12 At the nearest river, lake, or stream, dunk the entire bucket, fill it with a shower's worth of water, and screw on the lid.

13 Set your new solar shower in a spot where it will get a few hours of continuous sun.

14 When you get back to camp, find a thick branch or a spot between two trees and hoist the bucket about 7 feet off the ground.

15 Open the ball valve, lather, rinse, and repeat.

MAKE A SURVIVAL KIT

In unexpected situations, a survival kit can literally be a lifesaver. Survival kits come in all shapes and sizes. The emphasis of this particular kit is to ensure the availability of a large amount of drinking water, and to provide sterilization and care for open wounds, immobilization for broken bones, and methods for starting a fire in a variety of conditions. With it, you'll also be able to secure emergency shelter, hunt for your own food, and guide yourself to safety.

DIFFICULTY LEVEL:
Weekend Warrior

MATERIALS:

32-ounce PBA-free, wide-mouth plastic water bottle

8 water-purification tablets (Katadyn Micropur, for example)

52-by-82-inch aluminized polyester emergency blanket

1 pen

6 feet medical tape, wrapped around pen

6 feet duct tape, also wrapped around pen

Parachute cord (25-foot roll)

3-inch buck knife with LED light

3-foot-by-1-inch flat nylon webbing with buckle

1-ounce bottle SPF 30 sunscreen

1-ounce bottle Dr. Bronner's pure organic soap

1-ounce bottle isopropyl rubbing alcohol

5 alcohol wipes

3-by-3-inch gauze pads, kept sterile in Ziploc bag

Quart-size Ziploc bag

1-ounce tube Neosporin

6 extra-strength acetaminophen pills

2 antidiarrhea pills (bismuth subsalicylate)

2-by-3-inch patch moleskin

Stainless-steel snare wire (10-foot roll)

8-pound-test fishing line and needle (120-foot roll)

6 size-10 bait hooks

6 size-5 split-shot removable weights

Waterproof match container

15 waterproof, windproof matches

Cigarette lighter

Magnesium fire starter

All-in-one compass, whistle, thermometer, magnifying glass, mirror, and LED light (for example, the Coghlan Six-Function Whistle)

INSTRUCTIONS:

These supplies fit perfectly into a 32-ounce water bottle and weigh less than 2 pounds. The following are recommended uses for the items in the kit. This kit will aid one to four people.

1 The 32-ounce water bottle is an ideal container to transport, and purify, a large amount of water using either the 4-hour purification tablets or by boiling it over a campfire using the method described on page 46.

2 The emergency blanket can be used to reflect heat back to the body. Use tape to secure it over a person's head, feet, and hands. It can provide shade, or reflect the heat of a campfire on to a person or into a shelter. Draped over a cord strung between two trees, it can form a waterproof tent. With edges taped to hold it in place, it can be used as a waterproof, windproof poncho. It can also be used to collect rainwater or, framed with sticks, as a signaling device.

3 The buck knife has an almost unlimited number of uses. Cut green branches to make a lean-to. Clean fish. Cut a parachute cord to make a bow or snares. Cut and rough up kindling for a fire. Drive it into solid ice to get handhold. The built-in LED light is equally versatile.

4 The nylon webbing can be used as a tourniquet, an arm sling, or together with two sticks as a splint for a broken leg. It can also simply be used to haul firewood.

5 The sunscreen, of course, is to protect yourself from UV rays, which can be brutal at high elevations. If you're at elevation, the sun's rays become 8 percent to 10 percent more damaging for every 1,000 feet gained. Snow in the mountains? Triple threat. Wear your sunscreen.

6 Soap and simple hygiene can go a long way toward fighting disease. Soap and water are also the most effective way to clean a wound. Wash your hands often, especially before and after handling raw foods or redressing bandages. Wash knives and instruments after use.

7 Rubbing alcohol can be used to clean wounds and as fuel to help start fires. The same goes for alcohol wipes.

8 Use gauze to cover an open wound, or pull it apart to help start a fire.

9 A Ziploc bag can be used to store all of the contents of the survival kit or to carry additional purified water.

10 Neosporin helps prevent infection and promotes healing. It can also be applied to chafed skin that would otherwise prevent you from walking.

11 Tylenol or similar painkillers, by doing their job, may allow you to get some much-needed sleep.

12 If you've had some tainted food or water, antidiarrhea pills will help you absorb nutrients, water, and salt from nontainted food and speed your recovery.

13 If you feel blisters on your feet, cut a piece of moleskin and cover them up. It will stop the abrasion and keep you moving.

14 Use snare wire to trap small and medium-size game. You can also use snare wire to repair your gear or prepare food. To cook with it, just thread your food onto the wire and string it across the fire between two sticks.

15 Parachute cord can be used for just about anything. Tie it between two trees and drape the emergency blanket over it to make a quick shelter, or use it to lash pine poles together and make something more substantial. Make a bow, snare, or bolo to hunt game. Hang food out of animals' reach. Make a clothes-drying line.

16 Each water-purification tablet can treat a liter of water or can be ground up with a little water to clean a wound.

17 Fishing line and a needle can be used to suture a gaping wound, but—hey—it's also good for fishing! Cut your long line into three parts to triple your chances for a nice meal. After you're done fishing, you can use your line to redirect any water leaking into your tent. Just hook the line into the fabric at the leak, secure the other end away from your sleeping bag, and the drips will run down the line instead.

18 Use local insects as bait on the bait hooks. Scour the bushes around the water source and grab whatever is alive. That's what the fish are eating. If you're somewhere with soil, try the old standby and dig for worms.

19 Attach a split-shot weight 3 feet from the top of the bait hook and let it sink to the bottom. Tie the fishing line to a stick and wedge the stick between some rocks. Let the fish swallow the bait, and don't waste your time watching the line. You should be out gathering wood or setting snares.

20 Use your pen to leave messages for those searching for you. Tell them where you're going or where you can be found. Date the note. Out of paper? Use bark or duct tape. Leave notes at strategic points such as trail forks, gates, or fences.

21 Use medical tape to hold gauze in place or to close or cover wounds, if you have to.

22 Duct tape is another item with a long list of uses. Repair clothes. Strengthen the corners of your emergency blanket or fasten it with tape to create a poncho. Close wounds. Cover a bandage to create a dirt-proof layer. Repair your tent. Fix your shoe. Stop a leak. Make a label. Post a sign.

23 Waterproof matches work well in wet weather. You can light them wet, and once lit they will not go out even if completely submerged. They make a great backup for your regular lighter.

24 Use the lighter in dry conditions and save your matches for a wetter emergency. Also use it to melt the cut ends of parachute cord to keep them from fraying.

25 To give your kindling a boost, make a pile of magnesium shavings big enough to cover a quarter. Set dry leaves and twigs around the shavings and scrape the dull edge of your knife against the sparking insert to ignite.

26 The all-in-one compass is a guide, a whistle, and a mirror for signaling and grooming. It also has an LED, handy for quick lighting needs.

SURVIVE THE UNEXPECTED

Be prepared for any situation. As the old saying goes, "An ounce of prevention is worth a pound of rescue helicopter." The best way to avoid trouble is to do some thoughtful planning up front. Here are a few steps to take.

DIFFICULTY LEVEL: Car Camper

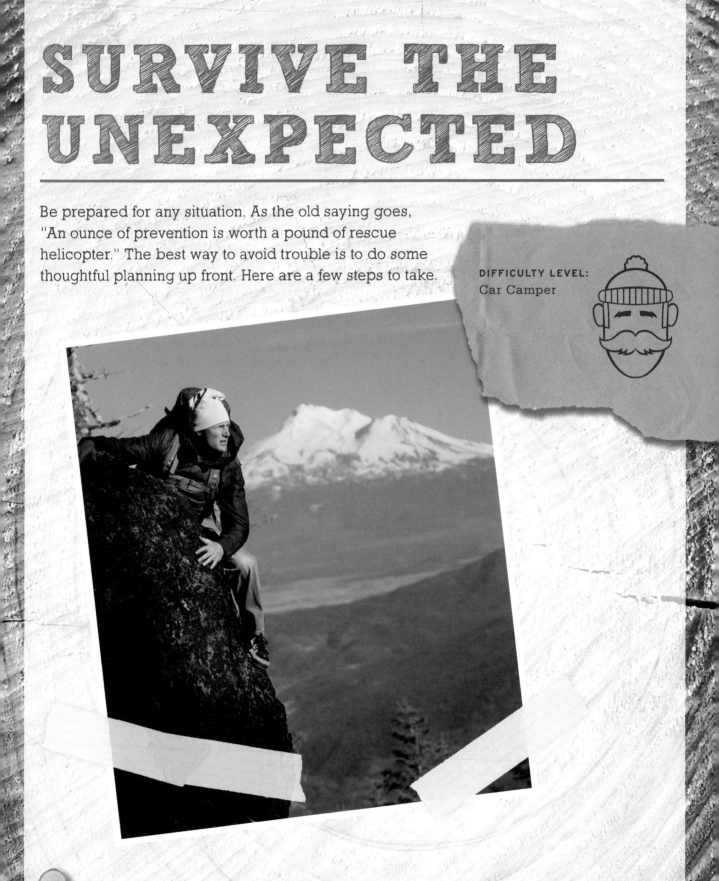

INSTRUCTIONS:

MAKE A WILDERNESS PLAN

The first thing you should do before heading out is to file a wilderness plan with a family member or a good friend. Let them know where you'll be going, what your route and itinerary will be, and when you'll be back. Update them, as soon as possible, if your plans change en route, and at the end of your journey. If they don't hear from you, they'll know where to send the search party.

FOR EACH KID, A KIT

Teach your kids early on to use a compass and map. Once they understand the skills, give each of your kids a mini survival kit outfitted with a map of the area, a compass, flashlight, pocketknife, water bottle, water-purification tablets, whistle, signaling mirror, warm clothes, and emergency rain gear. When they're old enough, teach them how to safely build and put out a campfire, and then include matches and a lighter in their kits.

ALWAYS KNOW WHERE YOU ARE

Always use a USGS or other good-quality topographic map when you're in the backcountry. Check the map often. Keep track of how long you've been hiking and in which direction. Mark your position at regular intervals.

DON'T TAKE SHORTCUTS

Catch yourself in those moments when you think it'd be quicker to jump across that rocky ravine rather than take the longer way around, or you're about to make a few more cuts with the axe you've noticed is dull. Don't do it. That's when accidents happen. Keep your gear and your judgment in tip-top shape and they won't let you down.

WHEN THE UNEXPECTED HAPPENS

Sometimes the unexpected happens even when you've taken every precaution to avoid it. First, look at the situation and accept what's happened. Your kid has a broken arm? You're completely lost? OK—there's no changing it now. The sooner you accept it, the sooner you can start improving the situation. Second, size up the situation.

What needs to be done? A broken arm will need a splint. Is night approaching? You'll need a shelter. Did you fall into a creek? You'll need a fire to stay warm and dry off. These are the basic needs for survival: water, shelter, a fire, first aid, food, and a way to signal for help. As soon as you've identified your needs, get busy meeting them. If you have less than 2 hours of daylight, start to gather wood, build a fire, and arrange a shelter. Staying focused on the task is not only productive; it's a morale booster. If you're with your family, give everyone a task.

IF YOU'RE LOST, STAY PUT

A moving target is a harder to find than a stationary one. Moreover, moving burns calories and increases your need for water and your risk of injury. Use your energy to stock-pile firewood, shore up your water supply, and signal for help. Damp wood or green foliage on a roaring fire makes great smoke.

IF CONFRONTED BY AN ANIMAL, DON'T RUN

Wear a bell or make noise while hiking. Most animals will gladly avoid you unless you're near their young. If you are confronted, don't run. Keep your eyes on the animal, stand your ground, or slowly back or sidestep away without turning your back to the animal. If a female bear protecting her cubs charges, calmly back away. If mountain lion or male bear threatens you, stomp your feet, throw rocks, fight back. You don't want it to think you're an easy target.

IMPROVISE

A jacket works as a signaling device. A folded magazine makes a good splint. A maxi pad makes a good bandage. Almost anything you have can do double-duty as something else.

ABOVE ALL, DON'T PANIC

Take comfort in the great likelihood that no matter where you are, help is no more than a few days away.

IDENTIFY EDIBLE AND POISONOUS PLANTS AND BUGS

The great outdoors is teeming with edible plants and bugs. Whether you're in an emergency situation or just interested in adding some wild plants and bugs to your camp stew, there's power and satisfaction in knowing which ones will sustain you and which will do you in.

DIFFICULTY LEVEL:
Backwoodsman

You'd be surprised at how many insect species are edible—about 1,500! That's more than enough for dinner. Insects are protein-rich, packed with vitamins and minerals, and many of them are downright tasty. You can eat them raw, but washing and cooking them will improve the taste and also kill off any parasites that hard-shelled insects can carry. The easiest and tastiest way to cook them is to sauté them in oil over high heat for 10 to 15 minutes.

One warning: Eating from the wild can be a thrill, but misidentifying a poisonous plant or bug can wreak havoc on your body or even kill you. Study well, choose wisely, and only eat specimens if you're 100 percent sure they're safe. See the Resources section (page 159) for some good websites to consult for proper identification.

Avoid eating bugs from urban areas. Their bodies can hold concentrated pesticides at dangerous levels. When in the wild, stay away from bugs that have a strong odor or bright color, and also ones associated with spreading disease, such as ticks, mosquitoes, and flies.

INSTRUCTIONS:

COMMONLY FOUND EDIBLE PLANTS:

Here is a list of the top 25 edible plants commonly found in North America. Search online for images and further details. Remember that even edible plants can pose risks if they're growing in an environment polluted by chemicals, heavy metals, or livestock waste, or if they're afflicted with fungi. Do your research and inquire locally.

Amaranth
(Amaranthus retroflexus)
This plant can be found on every continent. The entire plant is edible. Boil it for a minute or two for best results, or eat it raw.

Arrowhead *(Sagittaria latifolia)*
This plant grows in shallow wetlands and produces a potato-like root. Peel and roast it whole or cut it up and roast it to make fries. The plant gets it name from its large, three-pointed leaves. Also look for the three-petaled white flower with the yellow center.

Bulrush *(Scirpus lacustris)*
Found in freshwater marshes all over North America, this plant's root, stem, and seeds can be eaten raw or boiled.

Cattails *(Typha latifolia)*
Found the world over crowding the edges of wetlands, cattails provide edible roots. Peel away the outer layers of the shoots, rinse them in clean water, and eat raw or cooked.

Chicory *(Cichorium intybus)*
This is another plant found throughout North America. The blue and white flowers are delicious raw, as are the young leaves. Give the roots a quick boil before eating.

Clover, white and red
(Trifolium repens, pratense)
Both red and white clover can be found almost everywhere—even in your front lawn. All parts of the plant can be eaten. Dry the flowers for tea. The seeds, leaves, and roots can be eaten raw, though boiling the leaves for 5 to 10 minutes in saltwater makes them easier to digest.

Common chickweed
(Stellaria media)
You can find this little plant almost everywhere. The entire plant is edible raw. Look for the tiny white flower with five double-bladed petals at the center of each clump of leaves.

Curled dock *(Rumex crispus)*
Found around the globe, these bright red 3-foot-long stalks should be peeled and boiled to remove any bitter taste before eating.

Dandelion *(Taraxacum officinale)*
Yes, that weed in your garden is actually an incredibly healthy food source. The leaves are great in salads. The flower petals can be used to make dandelion wine. The ground and roasted roots are used to make a caffeine-free infusion called dandelion coffee. The whole plant is edible.

Field pennycress
(Thlaspi vulgaris)
Another worldwide find, this plant has leaves and seeds that can be eaten raw or boiled.

Fireweed
(Epilobium angustifolium)
This purple flowering plant can be found throughout the Northern Hemisphere and is best eaten when the leaves are young. The flowers and seeds have a peppery taste, while the stalk is slightly bitter.

Kelp *(Alaria esculenta)*
Kelp is a sea-based food found all over the planet. Drag some ashore, rinse it off with freshwater, and eat as much as you like. The leafy part is more nutritious and palatable, but the whole plant is edible.

Lambsquarters
(Chenopodium berlandieri)
Another "weed" that can be found almost everywhere, the leaves and stems can be eaten raw in salads, cooked like spinach, dried, frozen, or canned. You can even grind the seeds into flour for a back-woods pizza.

Plantain (Plantago species)
This is not the banana-like plantain that you may be thinking of. It's a broad-leafed plant that can be found primarily in wet areas like bogs but also in some alpine coastal areas. Eat the young leaves raw.

Prickly pear (Opuntia species)
Found throughout the Americas, this cactus yields both edible pads—the spiny, paddle-shaped segments that form the plant itself—and fruit, the "pears" that grow from the pads. Young pads tend to be the most succulent. Cut off the spines, roast the pads, and peel away the outer layer before eating them. The pears can be eaten raw like an apple; just remove the spines and peel the skins first.

Purslane (Portulaca oleracea)
Although it's known primarily as a weed here in the United States, purslane's thick, slightly sour leaves are eaten as a vegetable in much of the world. Purslane was purportedly one of Gandhi's favorite foods, and you too can share in its tastiness. Eat it raw as salad, or cooked like spinach.

Sea lettuce (Ulva lactuca)
Found in every ocean, this seaweed variant is both healthy and delicious.

Just rinse it with freshwater, if possible, and let it dry. Why not add it to the fish you just caught with your PVC Fishing Pole (page 94)!

Sheep's sorrel (Rumex acetosella)
This common weed favors moist fields, grass, and woodlands. The narrow leaves have a zesty lemon flavor.

Spring beauty
(Claytonia caroliniana)
These plants feature pink-streaked, white flowers and grow in moist woodlands. The bulb is the edible part. Pull it up, wash it off, and eat it cooked or raw.

Watercress (Nasturtium officinale)
As the name suggests, this plant grows near running water. Look for it next to streams and riverbanks. You can eat this green raw. Just break off the stem and rinse in cold water.

White mustard (Synapis alba)
Don't be fooled by the name. This common plant has edible yellow flowers, seeds, and leaves. Try squeezing it on your hot dog!

Wild Leek (Allium tricoccum)
The stems look like green onion and the plant has a strong garlic smell. Look for it deep in the forest in the early spring. Eat the leaves and bulbs raw, steamed, fried, or baked.

Wild onion (Allium stellatum)
This plant can be found on rocky slopes, in forests, and on prairies. It's just like the one found in the produce section of your grocery store. Simply boil the bulb with some salt.

Wild rice (Zizania aquatica)
Grows in shallow lakes or slow-moving streams along the Atlantic and Gulf Coasts and the Saint Lawrence River. It averages 3 to 4½ feet high. The stems, grains, and roots are all edible. Do not eat it if the grains are covered with pink or purplish blotches. These indicate the presence of a highly toxic fungus.

Wood sorrel (Oxalis species)
Sorrel is easily recognized by its three clover-like leaves and its five-petaled white or light purple flowers. The leaves have a bright, tart taste when eaten raw. The roots can be boiled for better digestion.

COMMONLY FOUND POISONOUS PLANTS:

Even more important than identifying edible plants is the ability to identify poisonous ones. Below is a list of plants to avoid. For more information on poisonous plants, consult the Resources list on page 159.

Autumn crocus
(Colchicum autumnale)

Black locust
(Robinia pseudoacacia)

Bleeding heart *(Dicentra formosa)*

Buttercup *(Ranunculus species)*

Cherry tree leaves (both wild and cultivated) *(Prunus serotina)*

Daphne *(Daphne mezereum)*

Elderberry *(Sambucus canadensis)*

Elephant ear
(Alocasia and Colocasia species)

Foxglove *(Digitalis purpurea)*

Golden chain *(Laburnum species)*

Hyacinth *(Hyacinthus orientalis)*

Iris *(Iris species)*

Jack-in-the-pulpit
(Arisaema triphyllum)

Jasmine berries
(Jasminum tortuosum)

Jimsonweed (a.k.a. thorn apple)
(Datura stramonium)

Larkspur *(Delphinium species)*

Laurels, rhododendrons, azaleas
(Rhododendron species)

Lily of the valley
(Convallaria majalis)

Mayapple
(Podophyllum peltatum)

Mistletoe
(Phoradendron flavescens)

Monkshood *(Aconitum napellus)*

Moonseed
(Menispermum canadense)

Oak *(Quercus species)*

Oleander *(Nerium oleander)*

Poison hemlock
(Conium maculatum)

Red sage *(Lantana camara)*

Rhubarb leaves
(Rheum rhaponticum)

Star of Bethlehem
(Ornithogalum umbellatum)

Water hemlock *(Cicuta maculata)*

Wild daffodil
(Narcissus pseudonarcissus)

Wisteria *(Wisteria species)*

Woody nightshade
(Solanum dulcamara)

Yew *(Taxus baccata)*

Mushrooms

Yes, they can be tasty. But in certain families, the delicious ones can be difficult to distinguish from the death dealers. If you're interested, learn from an expert. If you're casually dabbling, steer clear of them all.

INSTRUCTIONS:

COMMONLY FOUND EDIBLE BUGS:

When in doubt, remember this little saying:

Red, orange, yellow,
forget this fellow.
Black, green, or brown,
wolf it down.

So where do you find these delectable creepy crawlies? Look for larvae and grubs in cool, damp, confined places. Check under rocks, under the bark of fallen trees (or under the fallen trees themselves). You can find grasshoppers and other flying insects in open fields. They're easier to catch in the morning before they warm up. Harvest ants and termites by poking a stick into their nest. Give them a few seconds to swarm all over the stick and then pull it out. Block the other entrances to the nest so that you can harvest from a single exit point. Eat them off the stick. Look for maggots on damp, decaying material. You'll find earthworms under rocks and in warm, moist soil. Soaked ground forces them to the surface.

I've included here the most commonly found edible bugs, with a few tips on how to prepare them.

Agave worms
Yes, this is the same one that you may have seen in tequila bottles. Eat them raw or sauté them for a tasty addition to any meal.

Flying ants
Roast with lime juice and a touch of salt and they'll taste like pork rinds.

Honeypot ants
Eat them raw. Their abdomens are bursting with a sweet, honey-like nectar.

Leaf-cutter ants
Toast slightly in a pan and eat them by the handful. They taste like bacon and pistachios.

Lemon ants
Eat raw or boil them briefly. You guessed it—they taste like lemon.

Bees
Roast them and then grind them into flour. Bee bread, anyone?

Caterpillars
Remove the heads, squeeze out and discard the innards, then fry what's left with a little lemon or throw them into your favorite stew.

Cicadas
Catch them just after they molt, remove the wings, and sauté. They go great with vegetables.

Cockroaches
This is the most-devoured insect on the planet. Sautéed, toasted, or fried, they have a creamy taste and texture.

Crickets
Almost as popular as cockroaches, they can be boiled, sautéed, roasted, or fried.

Dragonflies
Remove the wings, heads, and legs and fry them in oil.

Dung beetles
Sure, they eat dung, but they're tasty just the same. Think of them as mushrooms with legs. Try them roasted or fried.

Earthworms
Soak them in water or damp cornmeal for 24 hours to purge their digestive tracts. Eat them raw or dip them in milk, roll them in cornstarch, and fry.

Grasshoppers
Slow roast and top with garlic, salt, and lemon juice.

Hornworms
Fry them up. They go great with green tomatoes.

June bugs
Both the larvae and the adults are delicious. Roast and eat them like popcorn.

Locusts

Remove the heads, wings, and legs. Sauté them in butter and add them to any meal.

Maggots

Wash and cook them before eating.

Mealworms

Rinse them in water, then fry, boil, grill, or sauté. You can find them almost anywhere, and they're very tasty.

Midge flies

Collect as many as you like and then mix them with sugar and flour. Press the resulting mixture into tasty cakes.

Scorpions

Remove the poison sack and the stinger by cutting off the tail. Then dip them in milk, then cornstarch, and then sauté them in butter. They taste like crabs or tiny lobsters.

Tarantulas

Believe it or not, you can actually eat these hairy monsters. Boil them to remove the hair and then deep-fry.

Termites

Eat them raw. They have a crunchy, nutty taste.

Bon appétit!

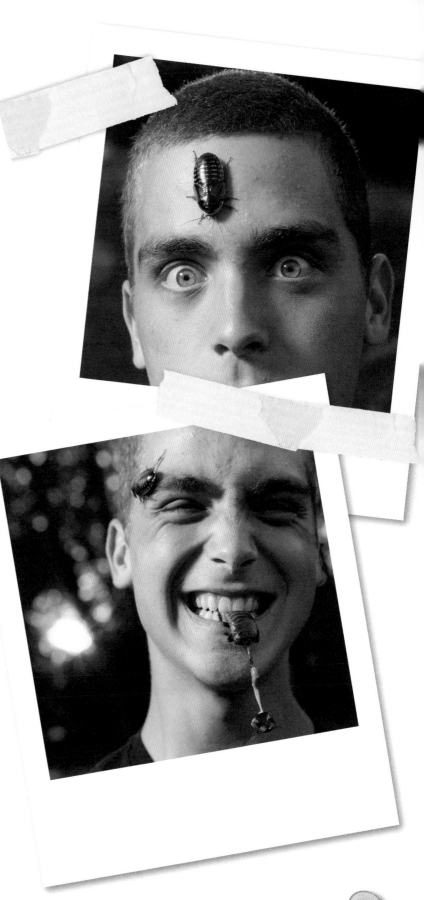

BOIL WATER IN A PLASTIC BOTTLE

Let's say that you're out camping. It's gorgeous. You've got everything you need: a beautiful view, a glowing fire, and your sheepskin-lined Crocs. Your kids are even nestled into their new Hello Kitty sleeping bags. With your mouth full of s'mores, you ask your honey for a bottle of water. "Hummy, cah do pasch da wahma?" you tenderly ask. And somehow she understands you—but not why you're asking. "I thought you had the water," she says as her eyes fill with panic. You're a two-day hike from anywhere, and your supply is all used up. Will you die of thirst? Will your children have to lick dew from blades of grass? No, because you bought this book and you know exactly what to do.

DIFFICULTY LEVEL:
Car Camper

MATERIALS:

Plastic PET or PETE water bottle (These are the thin-walled, clear bottles that water typically comes in. Any size will do.)

Water from the nearest stream or puddle

Aluminum foil

Fire with hot coals

Note: Boiling water is the surest and most effective method to destroy microorganisms, including disease-causing bacteria, viruses, protozoa, and parasites.

According to the Wilderness Medical Society, water temperatures above 160°F (70°C) kill all pathogens within 30 minutes, and if the temperature is above 185°F (85°C), within just a few minutes. In the time that it takes for the water to reach the boiling point (212°F or 100°C) from 160°F (70°C), all pathogens will be killed, even at high altitude where water boils at a lower temperature.

INSTRUCTIONS:

1 Grab your plastic bottle (or bottles) and head for the cleanest water source you can find. A stream is ideal, but any old puddle will do if it's an emergency.

2 The idea is to fill the bottle with water so that there is absolutely no air left in it. The water will keep the plastic from melting, so any air bubble creates a spot where melting plastic could cause the bottle to burst. If possible, fill and cap the bottle underwater. Barring that, fill the bottle a little beyond full, so that the water forms a meniscus at the top. That's when the surface of the water forms a little dome above the edge of the container. See image **a**.

3 Pour a little water into the cap and, in one motion, place it on the bottle and screw it down while giving the bottle a gentle squeeze. A little water should flow out of the bottle as you're tightening the cap. You should not have ANY air in the bottle.

4 Turn the bottle upside down. Do you see any tiny little bubbles floating to the top? You do? Start over. There should be no bubbles whatsoever.

5 How about now? OK—good. If you have some aluminum foil, fold it so that it's four layers thick and squeeze it tightly to cover the entire cap. This will prevent the cap from melting due to air trapped between the threads, which can happen on rare occasions. See images **b** and **c**.

6 Head over to your fire and make a cup holder–size indentation in the coals to hold the bottle. Move some logs into place to support the bottle so it won't fall over. See image **d**.

7 Place the bottle vertically into the indentation you made in the coals. See image **e**.

8 Let the bottle sit for 4 to 5 minutes and come to a low boil. Remarkably, the water will absorb the heat so that the plastic won't melt. When you start seeing small bubbles rising up along the inside of the bottle, remove it from the fire and let it cool. See images **f** and **g**.

a

START A FIRE WITHOUT A MATCH

When you stop and think about it, matches are pretty amazing. A flick of a wrist gives you an instant flame. But what if yours get wet, lost, or used up? Are you out of luck? Nope. There are several match-free ways to start a fire. Here are some of my favorites. Use these methods for emergencies or just to score some serious style points.

Employ any of these methods with the "fire nest" of a basic campfire structure, as described in "Build the Perfect Fire" on page 14, and you'll be in business.

DIFFICULTY LEVEL:
Car Camper

MATERIALS:

Dry grass or leaf litter

Steel-Wool Method

    1 pad fine steel wool

    9-volt battery

Flint-Stick Method

    2 cotton balls

    Flint stick with scraper (available at most camping stores)

Magnesium Method

    2 cotton balls

    Magnesium block with embedded flint striker (also available at most camping stores)

TOOLS:

Pocketknife

INSTRUCTIONS:

STEEL-WOOL METHOD

1 Make a small, volcano-shaped mound of dry grass or leaf litter.

2 Pull the steel wool apart to form a loose sphere a little bigger than a golf ball.

3 Place the steel wool in the depression at the top of your leaf pile, bunching the leaf litter around it.

4 Rub the battery against the steel wool for about a second, and then put the battery in your pocket. The steel wool will start to spark and burn.

5 Blow onto the wool once and scoop the leaves on top of it as it begins to burn.

6 Instant fire!

FLINT-STICK METHOD

1 Make a small, volcano-shaped mound of dry grass or leaf litter.

2 Pull apart the cotton balls and place them into the depression at the top of your pile. See image **a**.

3 Point the flint stick toward the cotton balls at about a 45-degree angle. Using the scraper, scrape the flint in one quick motion so that the sparks fall onto the cotton. See images **b**, **c**, **d**, and **e**.

4 Nudge more grass or leaves onto the cotton as it begins to burn.

5 Another instant fire!

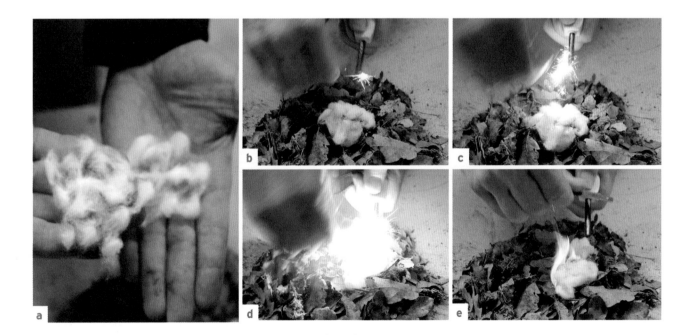

MAGNESIUM METHOD

1 Make a small, volcano-shaped mound of dry grass or leaf litter.

2 Pull apart the cotton balls and place them into the depression at the top of your pile.

3 Shave a pile of magnesium the size of a quarter onto the cotton. See image **f**.

4 USE CAUTION! The magnesium will erupt once the spark hits it. OK—using your pocketknife, scrape the flint and drop a spark on the magnesium.

5 Nudge the dry grass and leaves closer to the flames as the cotton burns.

6 Enjoy your fire and your woodsman cool points.

f

MAKE A TORCH

It happens all the time. You need to lead a tribe of head-hunters back through the jungle; or you need to crawl through the hidden door of a pyramid complex searching for the secret tomb; or you pitched your tent near Zombie Gulch and—dang it!—now a group of the undead have surrounded your campsite. What's the first thing you hear in any of these situations? "Grab the torches!" Ah, but where can you find good torches these days? Problem solved—here's how to make your own.

DIFFICULTY LEVEL:
Backwoodsman

MATERIALS:

1-inch aluminum pipe (2-foot section)

6 feet 2-inch-wide wire-reinforced Kevlar wicking

1 roll medical tape

3-inch wooden dowel

1-inch rubber stopper

Tube of high-temperature stove and gasket cement

Plastic or metal container with 3-inch-wide lid*

¼ gallon white camping fuel, paraffin oil, citronella fuel, or kerosene

FASTENERS:

Bottle of strong glue

Two 1-inch self-tapping steel screws

* Fuels will permeate untreated polyethylene. Make sure you use pretreated bottles.

TOOLS:

Tape measure

Felt-tip pen

Drill with a Phillips-head bit and $7/16$-inch bit

Vise (optional)

Lighter or matches

INSTRUCTIONS:

1 Mark two locations at one end of the pipe: one at ¾ inch from the edge of the pipe and another at 1¾ inches. See image **a**.

2 Drill a ⁷⁄₁₆-inch hole into the side of the pipe at each of the points you've marked, being careful to drill through only one side of the pipe. Have a friend help steady the pipe, or use a vise. See image **b**.

3 Draw a bead of glue between the holes. See image **c**.

4 Let's position the Kevlar wicking on the pipe. Start by lining up the edge of the wicking with the two holes, making sure each one is about the same distance from the edge of the wicking. Now rotate the pipe so that the holes disappear about ½ inch under the wicking. Tape the wicking down with medical tape. See image **d**.

5 Now wrap the wicking very tightly around the pipe.

6 Fold the end of the wicking under itself so that it wraps ½-inch past the red line and tape it down to hold it in place for now. See image **e**.

7 Now let's drill two holes into the wicking exactly over the holes in the pipe. Hold your tape measure over the wicking, in line with the red line, and mark at ¾ inch and at 1¾ inch. See image **f**.

8 OK—drill slowly through the Kevlar and into the previously drilled holes. Have a friend help steady the pipe, or use a vise. Again, don't drill through both sides of the pipe. See image **g**.

9 Push the 3-inch wooden dowel into the wick end of the pipe. The end of the dowel should be ½ inch inside the end of the pipe. See image **h**.

10 Place a self-tapping screw into each hole and screw them down as far as you can by hand.

11 Drive the screws the rest of the way into the wooden dowel with your drill and Phillips-head bit. Remove as much of the tape as you can. The rest will burn off. See image **i**.

12 With that done, let's make a grip on the other end of the pipe. Starting at the bottom, make three wraps of tape on top of one another before wrapping gradually and evenly up the pipe. When you've covered 8 inches of pipe, make three more wraps on top of each other and cut the tape. See image **j**.

13 Slide the grip end of the pipe into the rubber stopper as far as it will go. See image **k**.

14 Fill the ½-inch gap above the dowel on the other end of the pipe with high-temperature gasket cement, smooth it off evenly, and let it dry for at least an hour. This is important. It will keep fuel from leaking down into the part of the pipe where your hand is. See image **l**.

15 Fill the wide-lid container with fuel and let the wick end of the torch soak in it for about an hour. Prop the other end up in a corner, on a tree, or on a rock. Make sure it's stable. You don't want to be spilling kerosene everywhere. See image **m**.

16 When an hour is up, slowly pull out the torch, letting the excess fluid drip off. Seal the container.

17 Hold the wick end of the torch away from your body and light it. See image **n**.

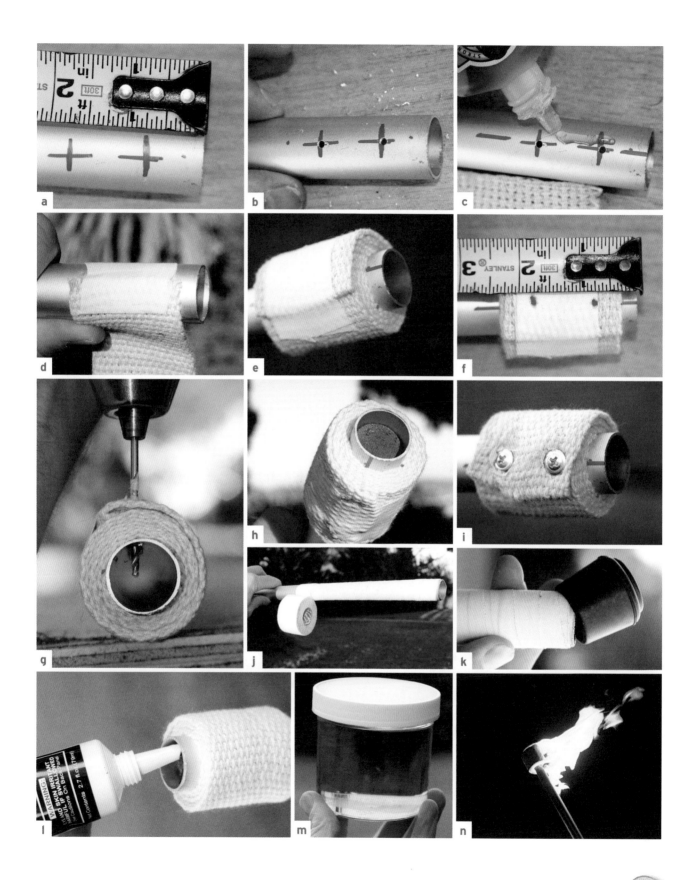

SNIPE HUNTING

Every group has its greenhorns, and what better way to initiate these young bucks than with the thrill of the hunt—the snipe hunt! The camaraderie, the chase, the anticipation of the catch, and finally the prize! Will your lucky newbies bag a bevy of cunning, elusive, fleet-footed snipes? There's only one way to find out! To the woods, men!

Note: Snipe hunting is a practical joke that involves taking newbie campers out on a wild goose chase and leaving them to find their way back to camp on their own. Use your judgment as to whether your newbies are up for this. I consider it an initiation rite appropriate for those older than 13 or 14, but definitely not for younger kids.

DIFFICULTY LEVEL:
Weekend Warrior

MATERIALS:

Brown paper grocery bags

Flashlights with low batteries

Fishing lures

INSTRUCTIONS:

① At some point during the day, mention to all of the campers, except the newbies, that this evening you're all going to go on a snipe hunt, wink, wink, nudge, nudge.

② Later in the evening, around the campfire, steer the conversation over to snipe hunting. Mention that this area is known for snipes and that this happens to be the perfect time of year. Recount the success of your last snipe-hunting trip. For example, "Yeah, after our last trip up here, we were eating snipe for days." You could, of course, take the other tack: "The snipe population's been down over the last couple of years, but I talked to the ranger, and this year they're making a comeback. I think we're gonna get lucky."

③ To rally the troops, yell, "Whoooo! Snipe hunt!" Then get up and grab enough brown paper bags to hand one out to everyone in the group.

4 Invariably the question, "What's a snipe?" will come up from one of your novice hunters. Just have everyone give differing descriptions as to what a snipe actually is. "It's a flightless bird." "It's hairy." "Well, it's actually furry." "It's really fast." "It has a long beak and pointy teeth." You get the idea.

5 Have everyone get a flashlight. If one of your newbies brought one, take it and give them the dim one, saying, "Take this one. They're scared of bright light." Meanwhile, keep your 3-foot Maglite on hand "to knock out the snipe once you've caught it."

6 Have everyone open their brown paper bags and roll the edges over so that they stay open. Explain that you'll set a lure in the bag and that later, when the snipe runs, they should close the bag and trap the snipe. Easy.

7 Continue to describe the wiliness and the cunning of the snipe as you hook a lure into the bottom of your newbies' bag. Don't forget to mention its delicate taste!

8 Describe the snipe in ever-more ridiculous detail as you head out into the woods to search for a fresh snipe trail. Throw out "facts" about how it gives birth to live young, has very small feathers, can run at lightning speed, is active at night, hides during the day (during which it looks brown, although it looks blue at night), has a beak, has fangs, and eyes that never blink, which are multi-colored like a husky's, etc., etc.

9 Don't forget to mention that snipes only exist in the region that you happen to be in (although there's also an Icelandic variety). Have you found the trail? Look for snipes tracks and other telltale signs of snipe activity.

10 Once you're in the woods, have the newbies place their bags on the trail, in the direction of the approaching snipes.

11 Take note of the position of bags, have everyone else spread out a little bit, and wait.

12 After a while, toss a stone in the nearby underbrush and intently whisper, "Did you hear that? That's a snipe, alright."

13 Have your newbies stay put while the rest of your party heads into the surrounding brush to "flush out snipes." Have the older kids turn their flashlights on and off to scare the snipes out of the brush. Make sure they're vocal about their snipe sightings. "There's one!" "Did you see that?" "There he goes!"

Toss more bits of bark and rocks here and there to make noise. Throw in some snipe calls. Pretty soon your newbies will start to see them, too. Snipes will be everywhere.

14 Run deeper into the forest, punch a hole into the bottom of your bag, and scream, "I got one." Run up to one of the in-the-know kids, who are still far away from the newbies, and celebrate. Make sure the snipe is rustling in the bag. Run back to show the new kids, but pretend to trip and fall far before you get there. Lament the fact that "he got away."

15 Make your way back to the newbies, still flushing snipes as you go, throwing bark, making noise, and pointing out the snipes that are heading their way.

16 What? They still haven't caught a single snipe? OK, have them turn on the flashlight and wiggle it as they shine it on the lure "because they attack shiny things."

17 Tell them to give it some time while you continue flushing, making noises, and turning flashlights on and off as you gradually head . . . back to camp.

18 Greet your would-be snipe hunters later that night and ask to see their catch. What? They came back empty-handed? The main thing is that they found their way back to camp. That's a successful snipe hunt!

19 In the morning, mention that you just happened to bring along enough snipe from last year's hunt to fry up some "snipe bacon and eggs" for the little kids.

COLLECT WATER FROM TREES

The next time you and your kids find yourselves standing in a forest clearing, ask them if they'd be able to make a cup of tea with only a plastic bag. They'll look at you like you're crazy. But it's possible! Here's the trick: trees spend all day exhaling water vapor. All you need to do is catch it.

DIFFICULTY LEVEL:
Weekend Warrior

a

b

c

d

INSTRUCTIONS:

1 To give yourself the longest window for water collecting, head out early in the morning. Find a chest-high branch with plenty of green leaves. Look for one without any pointy, broken branches that could puncture the plastic bag.

2 Wrap the trash bag around the end of the branch, fitting in as many of the smaller leaf-bearing branches as you can. See image **a**.

3 Close the open end of the bag evenly around the branch, making sure there's plenty of air in it, and secure it with a piece of wire. See image **b**.

4 If you find that the bag doesn't make an airtight seal, use your pocketknife to trim any bark or twigs that may be in the way. See image **c**.

5 Repeat this process with the other bag on a similar branch. See image **d**.

6 Spend 4 to 5 hours out and about, then head back and check your bags. You'll find that each one will contain up to a cup of "tree tea." Try some and pass it around. It will taste terrible! But, hey, you've just collected water out of thin air. And that knowledge may save your life one day.

WAR BONNET

Do you have a brave son or daughter who has passed great tests? A strong, just, and fearless leader, respected by all, and looked to for advice by the entire village (of younger siblings)? Then perhaps it is time to crown your young chief! Be sure to have a clever name ready. "I pronounce you . . . Chief Thunder Horse!"

DIFFICULTY LEVEL:
Backwoodsman

MATERIALS:

Adjustable baseball cap with Velcro closure

½ pound 13- to 15-inch brown-tip imitation eagle wing feathers (both left and right wing feathers)

Two 9-by-12-inch burgundy felt pads

Beaded headband with leather

2 ounces 3-inch white-tip plume feathers

1 ounce 3-inch black-tip plume feathers

Two 9-by-12-inch red felt pads

Beaded triple rosette necklace with fringe

Twelve 6-inch hand-painted imitation eagle fluffs

Two 2- to 3-inch replica black-bear claws

TOOLS:

Scissors

Tape measure

Sewing machine with spool of heavy-duty red thread

Pen

Large sewing needle

FASTENERS:

Jar of rubber cement

1 roll white athletic tape

200-foot roll cotton twine

100-yard spool 30-pound-test fishing line

Note: A good place to get materials is www.crazycrow.com/native-american-craft-supplies.

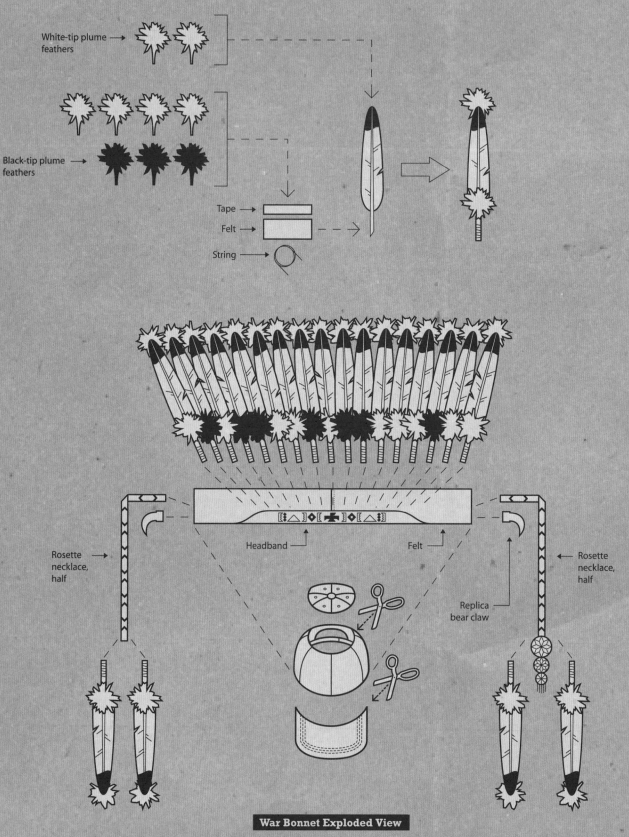

White-tip plume feathers

Black-tip plume feathers

Tape

Felt

String

Headband

Felt

Rosette necklace, half

Rosette necklace, half

Replica bear claw

War Bonnet Exploded View

INSTRUCTIONS:

1 Before you start, have a look at the **War Bonnet Exploded View** illustration to get an idea how the project will come together. To begin, cut a hole into the top of the baseball cap. To do this, fold the back half of the cap into the front and cut a semicircle out of the top, starting at the edge of the fold. Cut it 1 inch above the back of the hat so that it won't come apart when you adjust the Velcro. This hole will make the hat easier to work with. See image **a**.

2 Cut the visor completely off the hat, being careful not to cut any of the seams that hold the front of it together. See image **b**.

3 Pick out 17 of the best-looking right- and left-hand eagle wing feathers.

4 Fold the two burgundy felt pads lengthwise.

5 Place one pad inside the other to create a 23-inch-long felt pad. (The two pads should overlap by 1 inch.) See image **c**.

6 Use your sewing machine to sew all four layers of felt together, or sew them by hand. The stitch should be ½ inch from the edge of the outside piece of felt. See image **d**.

7 Using that stitch as a centerline, make a mark 9 inches out in both directions and cut off the ends of the felt there. The felt piece should be 18 inches long when you're done.

8 Place your beaded headband flush along the folded edge of the felt, making sure it's centered lengthwise.

9 Using your pen, draw a line onto the felt along the top edge of the headband. See image **e**.

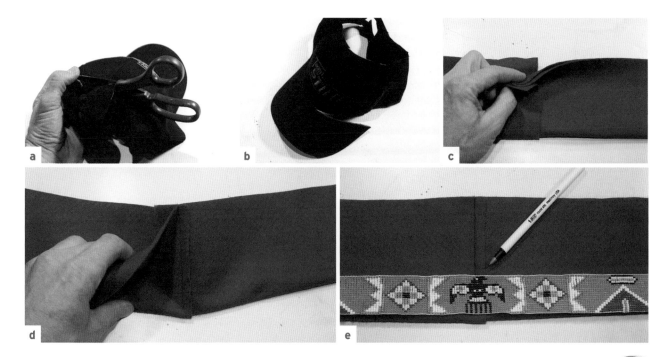

10 Let's apply rubber cement to the 34 eagle feathers. Cover an area on the underside of the feather 1 inch from its tip (not the quill end) and 1 inch wide (½ inch on either side of the center). Use a generous amount of cement. Be sure to keep the 17 left-hand feathers separate from the 17 right-hand feathers. (The top of a left-handed feather tilts to the left when you're holding it upright by the quill and looking at its front side.) See photo. Set aside to dry. See image **f**.

11 Now let's apply rubber cement to 68 of the white-tip plume feathers. On these, we'll be applying the cement to one side of the bottom of the feather (on the quill-point end). Coat it to about an inch up from the quill tip. Set these aside to dry.

12 Once all of the glue is completely dry, press the glued parts of the plume feathers onto the glued tips of the eagle feathers. Use two white plume feathers per eagle feather tip, putting one on either side of center. Do this for all 34 eagle feathers, again keeping the lefts and rights separate. See image **g**.

13 Cut a 2-inch-long piece of athletic tape and set it within easy reach.

14 Gather four white-tip plume feathers together so that the bottoms of their quills are all even. Then, holding the tape vertically, press the feathers into the upper-left corner of the tape so that the feathers lie perpendicular to the tape's length. See image **h**.

15 Take three black-tip plume feathers and press them into the tape on top of, and a little to the right of, the white feathers. See image **i**.

16 Wind the top ½ inch of the tape very tightly around the feathers, leaving the bottom 1½ inches of tape free.

17 Now let's attach those black-and-white plume feathers to an eagle feather. Hold the plume feathers, white-side out, against the bottom of the eagle feather and wrap the tape tightly around the quill. See image **j**.

18 Repeat this process for the 33 remaining feathers.

19 Cut both pieces of red felt, lengthwise, into six 3-by-12-inch strips.

20 Now snip the resulting strips at 2-inch intervals to create thirty-six 2-by-3-inch pieces.

21 Cut the bottom ½ inch off of all the feather quills.

22 In these next few steps we're going to wrap the bottoms of the eagle feathers with the felt pieces. Start by cutting a 2-foot piece of cotton twine and tying a loose overhand knot in it, 3 inches from one end. The knot should be loose enough to fit the felt-wrapped quill through later.

23 Now place the quill onto the edge of a piece of felt so that the feather is perpendicular to the 3-inch side. Leave ¾ inch of fabric below the end of the quill. See image **k**.

24 The idea here is to roll the felt very tightly around the quill, leaving the tail end on the back side of the feather.

25 Twist the leftover, ¾-inch end of the felt and fold it back upon the quill.

26 Now slip the felted end of the feather into the knot you made earlier and tie it off ½ inch from the bottom. Try to make the knot on the back side of the feather so that it's not visible from the front. See image **l**.

27 Wrap the long end of the twine around the felt about five or six times in the direction of the feathers and about two or three times back down to the bottom of the covered quill. Tie off the two ends of the string with a square knot. See image **m**.

28 Repeat Steps 22 through 27 with 32 of the remaining eagle feathers, setting aside one left-hand and one right-hand feather for further decoration.

29 All done? Good job! Now we're going to work on the two eagle feathers we set aside. These will be part of the special feathers hanging down on either side of the war bonnet. Let's start by grabbing the rosette necklace and wrapping a 2-inch-long piece of tape around the top of it (the part that would lie against the back of your neck were you to have it on). Wrap another 2-inch piece of tape just above the biggest medallion. See images **n** and **o**.

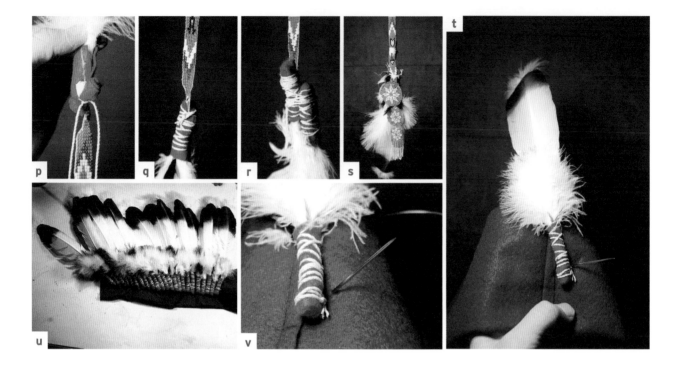

30 Cut through the middle of each piece of tape and set the two necklace pieces aside.

31 Take the one left-hand and one right-hand feather you set aside earlier and, with a 2-inch piece of athletic tape, attach six 6-inch imitation eagle fluffs tightly to the underside of each, at the bottom of the feather, making sure all of the quills point in the same direction.

32 Wrap a piece of red felt around one of the unfinished feathers as we did in Steps 22 through 27 but, as you fold the ¾-inch piece of felt over, include the end of the smaller piece of necklace. Orient the necklace so that it hangs straight down from the bottom of the feather. Secure with twine as before. See images **p** and **q**.

33 Grab a finished feather that's going to be on the same side of the bonnet as the one you just completed (i.e., left-hand or right-hand) and, using twine, tie the two together, facing in the same direction but staggered ½ inch apart. See image **r**.

34 Get the other feather you set aside earlier, finish it with felt, and tie it to another completed feather from the same side, offset ½ inch as in the previous step.

35 Again, using twine, attach these two feathers to the other necklace piece, just above the medallion. See image **s**. Let's set these special feathers aside.

36 Cut a 2-foot piece of fishing line, and thread 3 inches of it through the heavy-duty needle.

37 Now it's time to attach the feathers to the felt pad we finished in Step 9. Grab your best-looking left-hand feather. Place the bottom of the wrapped quill so that it just touches, and sits above, the line representing the top of the headband (the one you drew in Step 9). The bottom of the feather should sit ¾ inch to the right of the centerline and the top should tilt to the left across the centerline. See image **t**. See image **u** to get an idea of the tilt.

38 To sew the feather into place, start by punching up through the bottom of the felt, right next to the quill, ½ inch up from the underside of the felt. See image **v**.

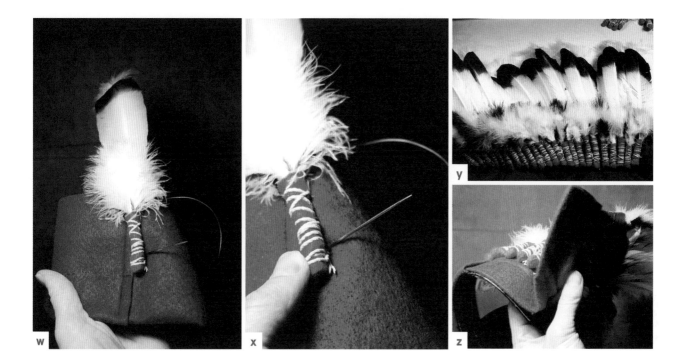

39 Loop once over the top of the wrapped quill and punch down through felt on the other side.

40 Flip the felt over and pull the needle so that you leave 3 inches of fishing line at the other end. Make one more loop over the top of the quill and pull the two ends of the fishing line tight, securing them with a square knot. See image **w**.

41 Flip the felt back over and adjust the feather as needed. This is the "keystone" feather, so make sure it's properly placed. It will influence the positioning of all the other feathers. Does it look like it will cover the center of the bonnet? OK—then attach it with fishing line, as before, ½ inch below the upper edge of the felt. See image **x**.

42 Using the same fishing-line sewing method, attach another left-hand feather snugly to the left of the center feather. Continue attaching left-handed feathers. The trick, as you work, is to rotate the top of each left-handed feather a little more to the left, while keeping the wrapped-quill ends snugly together and lined up on the line you drew above the headband. By incrementally rotating the feathers, they will lie perfectly when the bonnet is worn. See image **y**.

43 Attach the right-hand feathers in the same way. Line the bottoms up on the line you drew and place each wrapped end snugly against the previous one, checking for consistent feather placement near the tips. By the time you get to the third right-hand feather, it should be perpendicular to the edge of the felt. Continue attaching feathers while incrementally arching them to the right. If any feathers feel loose, add more stitching. If they're misaligned, take them off and reattach.

44 OK—it's almost powwow time. Center the completed felt onto the front of the baseball cap, feather-side out. At the center, the bottom edge of the felt should overlap the bottom edge of the cap by ¼ inch. See image **z**. At the sides of the cap, the felt should overlap by 1 inch.

a

b

c

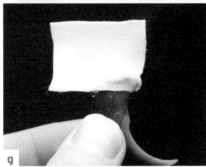

d

e

f

g

h

45 Now sew the felt to the hat, stitching just below the ends of the feathers. Make a 3-inch-long stitch on both sides of center, sewing each line twice. Leave the last 6 inches of felt on either side unsewn. See images **a** and **b**.

46 Center the beaded headband on the felt so that it overlaps the lower edge by ⅛ inch.

47 Sew the headband to the felt using a vertical line of stitches on both sides, 3 inches from center. Double up on these stitches, too. See image **c**.

48 Put the bonnet on your head, pulling the corners of the felt away from you and down toward the floor. Then place the bonnet on your table, exposing the fishing line–knotted back side of the felt. Now pull the ends of the headband out and, without flipping them over, move them to the back side of the felt so that the edges are flush. See image **d**. Sew the headband to the felt just before the leather. Do this for both the right and left sides of the headband. See image **e**.

49 Now let's grab the special feathers we set aside in Step 35. Take each set by the necklace ends and hold them to the sides of your head. Rotate them until both sets of feathers curl inward toward your body. The side of the necklace touching your head will be the side facing outward when you sew the necklace to the back side of the felt just above the headband, one on the left, and one on the right. See photo for placement. Go ahead and sew them. Be sure to double back on your stitching to ensure that it doesn't unravel. See image **f**.

50 Find your replica bear claws and grab a couple of 2-inch pieces of athletic tape. Set the base of the claw, pointy side down, against the middle of the tape. It should overlap about ¼ inch. Fold the tape in half so it clamshells over the bear claw. Do this for both claws. See image **g**.

51 Insert a claw into each open end of the felt, near the fold, so no tape can be seen. The claw tip should point in, toward the face when worn. Sew the ends of the felt closed, as close as possible to the base of the claw. Your stitching through the tape will hold the claw in place. Do the same for the other side. See image **h**.

52 Gather the tribe together and, on the mountain, by the tepee, under the bright stars of the new moon, light a fire, and have a coronation ceremony for your new chief.

WAR PAINT

In the old days, war paint was made from plants, clay, ashes, moss, animal fat, even duck dung. If your own pint-size brave wants to go raid the girls' tent or cabin, there's no need to poke around the edge of a duck pond for your supplies. Simple food coloring will do the trick.

If you want to go natural, try burnt cork (let it cool before applying!), cool ashes from last night's fire, or red clay if it's nearby. Mix with a little water and apply before hitting the warpath.

DIFFICULTY LEVEL:
Car Camper

MATERIALS:

5 Popsicle sticks, one for each of your colors

3½-ounce can hair-shaping cream or pomade (The Paul Mitchell Tea Tree shaping cream I used worked great. Check your local beauty supply store.)

5 small styrofoam cups, one for each of your colors

¾- to 1-ounce bottles food coloring in as many colors as you wish (I used black, red, blue, green, and yellow.)

TOOLS:

Knife

INSTRUCTIONS:

1 Using a Popsicle stick, scoop out a medium-size dollop of shaping cream or pomade that covers the bottom inch of the stick.

2 Place the cream-laden stick in a Styrofoam cup. Add 10 drops of food coloring to the cup and mix, gathering the now-colored shaping cream back on your stick when you're done. See image **a**. Repeat this for each of your other colors.

3 Cut the cups 1½ inch from the bottom with a sharp knife. See image **b**.

4 Now scrape the cream into the bottoms of the cups and line them up. See image **c**.

5 Applying war paint is easy. Just use your finger.

a

b

c

TRAIL BLAZING AND TRAIL MARKING

Let's say you find a trail to an amazing waterfall or a gorgeous lookout spot in some wild, remote location. How will you mark it to remember the way there next time? Sure, your GPS will come in handy. But if the batteries die or if you simply want to share the trail with others who happen to come across it, it's time to get back to basics. Think of this as OPS, the Old-school Positioning System.

DIFFICULTY LEVEL:
Car Camper

MATERIALS:

2- to 4-inch-diameter by 6-to-12-inch-long logs (You'll need one log for every 2 to 4 trail markers.)

1 can lead-free, fluorescent orange marking paint

1 box 16-penny, galvanized nails

TOOLS:

Tape measure

Long axe

Drill with ¼-inch bit

Hammer

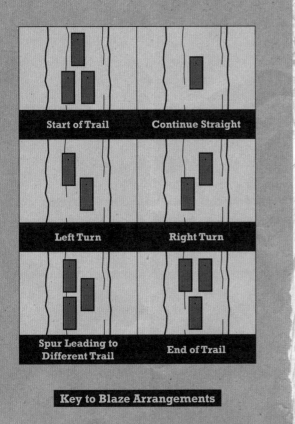

Start of Trail

Continue Straight

Left Turn

Right Turn

Spur Leading to Different Trail

End of Trail

Key to Blaze Arrangements

INSTRUCTIONS:

1 Cut several logs, lengthwise, into 1-inch-thick planks. The ideal blaze, or trail marker, should measure 2 by 6 inches. Let's start by making about 14 of them.

2 For each blaze, drill a centered, ¼-inch hole into the face of the piece 2 inches from the top edge.

3 Head out and arrange the blazes at key locations along the trail according to common trail-blazing symbols shown in the illustration. Put markers at points where the trail changes direction, or by marking "Straight Ahead" where the route is not obvious.

4 When marking, place blazes within 20 feet of the trail so they can be seen from a distance as hikers approach.

5 Spray one side of the blazes lightly with orange paint.

6 Mark the start of the trail with the pyramid-shaped arrangement by nailing blazes to a tree at eye level. Nail through the holes you drilled, leaving about a ½-inch gap between the tree and the blaze. This will preserve the blaze for years to come by allowing for tree growth.

7 When the trail heads out above the tree line, stack rocks into what are known as "cairns" or "ducks." These purposely placed piles look like nothing formed naturally and do a great job as markers.

8 To make a cairn, stack two, three, or more large, flat rocks on top of each other in order of descending size. Place them so that hikers can always see the next cairn from the current one. Since they usually mark a trail across an open expanse of rock, there's no need for cairns signaling "left" or "right." Here it's a matter of "connect the dots."

9 Place a few intermediary cairns as well, so that hikers can see two or three cairns ahead. This will add a level of backup in case any of the cairns are knocked over by high winds, snow pack, critters, and/or punk kids.

PRANKS!

Outdoor fun is even more fun when you pull a couple of good pranks. The pranks I've included here are versatile. They work at camp, around the house, or in the camp-ground. Prank a buddy. Prank a bully or a know-it-all. Just prank judiciously.

And be prepared to get pranked in return.

DIFFICULTY LEVEL:
Weekend Warrior

INSTRUCTIONS:

SNAKE ATTACK

Tie one foot of fishing line to a rubber snake and place it in the snack cupboard. Tape the other end of the line to the inside of the cabinet door. Put a little knot in the end of the fishing line so it doesn't slide under the tape. Now ask a buddy to do you a favor and grab you some pretzels. After you hear the scream, tell him to watch out for snakes. Snake sightings in the area have been on the rise!

HOT STRAW

Be a pal and grab your buddy a soda. Go ahead and put a straw in it for him, too. Before you do, though, put the straw in a bottle of hot sauce, holding your finger over the top of it as you pull the straw out. That's right—the straw will be full of hot sauce. Place it gently into the soda and deliver it to your bro. Stand back and watch him take a long, refreshing—"Wahhhh! Hot sauce!" Again, make sure to pull this on a buddy, not your friend's little kid.

MORNING REVEILLE

This one is good if you want to prank a bunch of people at once—but be careful. You may soon find a bunch of people out to prank you. Buy four cheap alarm clocks and set them so that one goes off every half hour starting at 4 a.m. Hide them in the rafters, under the bed, outside the door, or in someone's bag. The next day, ask your friends how they slept. If you want to take it to the next level, buy a few cheap plastic wristwatches with alarms and remove the bands. Remove the plastic covers from a couple of light switches around the room, set the alarms, and hide the watches in there. Replace the light covers. Let the sleeplessness begin!

THE ROCKY MAP

If you have a new hiker with you or just a friend you want to prank, tell them you'd like to give them the honor of carrying the map, a great privilege. Once they have their backpack on, put the map in the main compartment of their backpack. Even if you know where you're going, put some random map in there. As you do, put a good-size rock in their pack as well. It should be big enough to have some heft, but not so big that they'll immediately notice it. Check the map several times as you hike up the mountain, adding another rock each time. If they fall behind, tell them to keep up the pace!

When you reach your camp, help them take their pack off, and ask them to go get some firewood. While they're gone, remove the rocks and they'll never be the wiser. It works just as well going down the mountain!

SHORT-SHEETING A BED

Take the cover off the bed and remove the pillows. Grab the edge of the top sheet (near where the pillows were), pull it up toward the headboard, and tuck it underneath the mattress. Now grab the other end of the top sheet (from the foot of the bed) and fold it toward the head of the bed. Now put the cover back on the bed and fold the free end of the top sheet over the cover so it appears as before, put back the pillows, and wait for your buddy to slide in to bed. Whoops, they can't!

LARGE AND IN CHARGE

Buy a huge pair of underwear, write your friend's name on the waistband, and leave them hanging in the bathroom.

SHAVING CREAM SPECIAL DELIVERY

Grab a 9-by-12-inch manila envelope and fill it with shaving cream. Slide the open end under the door of your neighbors' cabin and pound on the door and scream that you're being chased by raccoons. When the lights go on, pounce on the envelope and run. The entire cabin will be ready for a shave.

FLAPPY DOORS

Tie parachute cord around the doorknob of one cabin and the one directly across from it, or two rooms across the hall from each other, leaving about 6 inches of slack. Then, you and a buddy pound on both doors at the same time yelling, "There's a skunk in there!" Watch as they keep opening and closing each other's doors.

DOUBLE STUF WITH FLUORIDE

Take Double-Stuf Oreos apart and replace the filling with toothpaste. Do this with all but a few of the cookies. Put all of the cookies back in the package keeping the non-minty ones at the front. Take the cookies to the campfire party, eat a couple and pass the package along. The first few people will enjoy a good cookie, then things will go all minty.

LOCKED OUT OF THE SOFA

Early in the morning, wake your friend and say, "Hey, where are the keys to the sofa? I'm locked out." Keep asking, saying things like, "You had the keys last. Where are they?" Who knows, you might get an answer that makes some sense.

WHISTLE TIPS

Get a whistle and a potato. Hollow out the middle of the potato along two-thirds of its length so that you can fit the whistle inside it. Estimate where the air will come out of the whistle and carve a hole into the top of the potato for the air to escape. Push the whistle into the potato. Does everything line up? OK—push the open end of the potato onto your friend's tailpipe. Woo-woooooooot!

GHOST FOG

Start a rumor that a strange "ghost fog" has been seen around camp. Maybe the ghosts can be seen rising out of the fog, or the fog turns people into zombies. Get creative with the story. Then hide out in the woods near the fire ring with a 5-gallon bucket of water and a hunk of dry ice and, when it gets dark . . . drop in the dry ice for some serious ghost fog!

COULDN'T HOLD IT

Place some duct tape under the opening of the sink faucet so that you cover the back three-quarters of the opening while leaving a sliver near the front open. When the next person uses the faucet, they'll get a stream of water right in the crotch!

SLUMBER LAND

Remove any alarm clocks from your neighbors' cabin and tape cardboard over the windows. What? They slept through breakfast and lunch? Bummer.

STEW, ANYONE?

Before your friend gets in the shower, unscrew the showerhead and stuff a couple of beef bullion cubes in it. Screw the showerhead back on. When he gets in the shower . . . beef stew!

OLD FAITHFUL

Freeze Mentos into ice cubes. When you go around with
your pitcher of soda to refill peoples' glasses, always make
sure to give them plenty of ice as well. Make sure to get
rid of all your ice cubes before they melt. When the ice
melts and the Mentos make contact with the carbonated
liquid, stand back and watch the soda fountains!

FREE MONEY

Super-glue some change to the ground where everyone
gets off the bus for camp. Watch with glee as the first kid
to notice tries to pry the change off the ground and holds
up the line. Hey, lemme off the bus!

SQUEAKY-CLEAN ORAL HYGIENE

Buy a toothbrush that looks like your buddy's. Borrow his
camera and have a friend take photos of you cleaning
the toilet with "his" toothbrush. Be sure to get some nice
close-ups of the action. Then later, when your buddy
is enjoying his photos, he'll see that his toothbrush is
famous!

KNOT SLEEPY

Grab a friend and tie your buddy's sleeping bag in a knot
while he's out. This is a two-man operation—one guy
pulls from each end. Throw the sleeping bag in the tent
and zip it up. Oops, it might take him a while to get to
sleep tonight!

FAKE SKIN AND BLOOD

If you've already read about keeping your food safe from bears (and bears safe from your food) on page 22, your camping trip should be bear-free. But sometimes kids need a little excitement. Here's where some fake skin and blood can come in handy. Jaws will surely drop as your son or daughter staggers into camp and tells the harrowing tale of their encounter with the 16-foot-tall grizzly. Then, to take it up a notch, stitch your kid's pseudo-wound up with fishing line as she tells her tale. Let the fainting begin!

DIFFICULTY LEVEL:
Car Camper

MATERIALS:

For the blood

16-ounce bottle light corn syrup

1-ounce bottle red food coloring

8-ounce tin cocoa powder

Popsicle stick or spoon

For the skin

1 drop red food coloring

¼ cup hot water

2 packets Knox unflavored gelatin

½ ounce cornstarch

2 Popsicle sticks

TOOLS:

For the blood

Small bowl

½-cup measure

1-tablespoon measure

1-teaspoon measure

One 6-fluid-ounce bottle, plus an (optional) extra

For the skin

1 small bowl

1 pocketknife

Needle with fishing line (optional)

INSTRUCTIONS:

FOR THE BLOOD

This recipe will yield about 4½ ounces of blood. Blood from gushing wounds tends to flow pretty fast, though. Are you sure you have enough? When in doubt, make a double batch.

1 Fill the bowl with ½ cup of light corn syrup.

2 Pour 2 tablespoons of red food coloring into the bowl. See image **a**.

3 Pour a teaspoon of cocoa powder into the bowl and mix the ingredients thoroughly. See images **b** and **c**.

4 Pour the blood into the 6-ounce bottle and save for later. See image **d**.

This blood is totally edible!

FOR THE SKIN

1 Add a drop of red food coloring to the bowl, pour in the hot water, and mix. Then add the two packets of gelatin and stir vigorously for 3 minutes and let sit for 10 minutes. See images **e**, **f**, and **g**.

2 Decide which arm will sport the wound. If you're doing this to your kid's arm, it's their call. If you're working on yourself, it will be easier if you choose your less-dominant side, i.e., your left arm if you're right-handed. Rub a little cornstarch (a moderate heap covering half a Popsicle stick) on your arm. This will help dry it out a bit so the fake skin will stick better. See image **h**.

3 After the gelatin has sat for 10 minutes, use the Popsicle stick to apply a thick layer to the survivor's forearm. See image **i**.

4 When you've got a good base of gelatin on, apply a thin layer of cornstarch. This will help the gelatin not be so sticky to the touch. Just pat the fake skin to remove the any excess cornstarch. See image **j**.

5 Press down firmly on the edges of the fake skin so that it blends seamlessly with the real stuff.

6 Now let's make some gnarly claw marks. Lay the edge of the knife against the fake skin and press down. Don't slice! Just push the blade slightly to the side to form the gash. Repeat to make four claw marks. See image **k**.

7 Again, apply some cornstarch to the gashes and pat away the excess. See image **l**.

8 OK—this is where things will start to look intense. Drip some of your freshly made blood into the wounds. Then smear more blood over the fake skin until no cornstarch is visible. See images **m** and **n**.

9 If you're camping, send your kid out with the bottle of fake blood so that he can pour the rest of it over his wound (and face!) before he comes screaming back into camp, recounting his ghastly bear tale.

10 Calm your child down and tell him not to worry, and that you'll have him stitched up in a jiffy. Pull out the needle and fishing line and get to work, being careful, of course, to stitch up the fake skin and not his actual arm.

11 Watch the other campers gasp in horror.

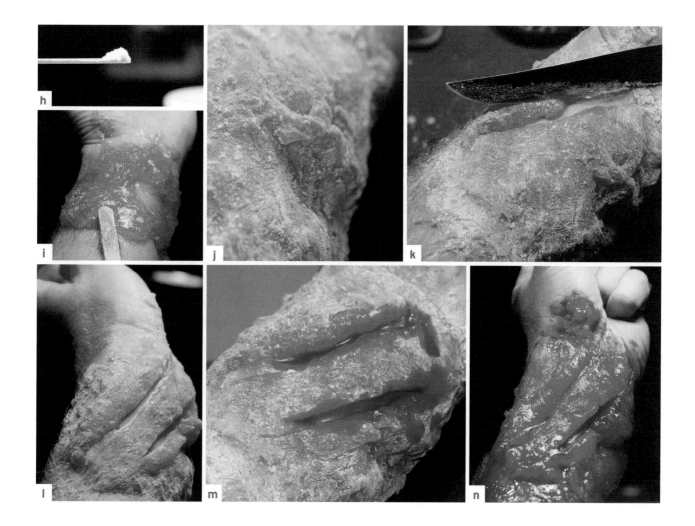

TENT-SIDE SHADOW PUPPET SHOW

Everyone knows tents are great for sleeping in, but did you know that they also make fantastic performance-art spaces? With a few simple props, your kids can put on quite a show, whether it be an Old West adventure or a new-school drama. So grab some s'mores, pull up a camp chair, and let the show begin!

DIFFICULTY LEVEL:
Car Camper

MATERIALS:

6 sheets letter-size printer paper

6 manila folders

Three 4-foot-long wooden dowels

1 bottle rubber cement

1 box brass-plated fasteners

Duct tape

TOOLS:

Computer   Scissors

Printer   X-ACTO knife

INSTRUCTIONS:

1 Print out six different characters readily identifiable by their silhouettes. I chose a cowboy, his horse, a bear, and a Native American woman. Wait, that's only four. OK, make two cowboys and throw in a snowboarder to keep things interesting. Just make sure that each silhouette fits on a letter-size piece of paper.

2 Attach the printed silhouettes to the manila folders using the rubber cement. Cardboard will work, too. It's just harder to cut. Position the cowboy and Native American woman so that you can cut them out of two layers of manila folder. This will give you two identical silhouettes with which you can create a puppet with a moveable body. See image **a**.

3 Using the scissors and the X-ACTO knife, if you need it for the details, cut the characters out of the manila folders.

4 Start with the two cutouts of the Native American woman. Cut the front silhouette in half at the hips and the back silhouette in half at the chest. After that, glue the fronts and backs together with rubber cement. You'll have a top and bottom piece for each character that overlap. Where they overlap, cut a small slit and join the pieces with a brass fastener. Now you have a puppet that moves! Trim any part of the back piece that sticks out beyond the edge of the silhouette when the top of the character is moved to one side or the other. See images **b**, **c**, **d**, and **e**.

5 Cut your wooden dowels in half and prepare two 2-inch pieces of duct tape.

6 Stick a piece of duct tape to the end of one of your cut wooden dowels. Half of the tape should be on the dowel, and the other half should be hanging free.

7 Attach the dowel to the puppet, just below the shoulders, using the free end of the tape. Press firmly. Put the other piece of tape on the other side of the dowel so that it mirrors the first. Again, press firmly. Trim any tape that protrudes beyond the puppet's edge. See images **f** and **g**.

8 Build your other puppets in the same way. If you feel like getting fancy, make a cowboy with a moveable arm that can tip his hat!

For nonmoveable puppets, skip Step 4.

9 Put the puppeteers in the tent, turn on the lights inside, and let them show you how the West was won! See image **h**.

PAN FOR GOLD

Just because the gold rush started over 150 years ago doesn't mean that all of the gold has been found. That's right—there's still gold in them thar hills! Here's how to find it.

DIFFICULTY LEVEL:
Car Camper

TOOLS:

Combination classifier sifting pan

Garrett Super Sluice gold pan

Folding shovel

14-inch gravity-trap gold pan

10½-inch piggyback gravity-trap gold pan

Tweezers

1-ounce plastic vial

Garret Gold Guzzler suction snuffer bottle

Note: For the best results, you'll need some good gear. You can find supplies online at www.goldfeverprospecting.com.

INSTRUCTIONS:

1 Find your panning spot. The ideal place to start is in a creek, downstream of boulders. That's where swirling gold settles onto the creek bed. See **Where to Pan** illustration.

2 Put the combination sifting pan in the Super Sluice pan and place it next to the stream. Dig sand and gravel from behind your lucky boulder and use this material to fill your nested pans half full.

3 Submerge the pans and their contents completely in water.

4 Holding the pans level under the water, slowly move them back and forth so the heavier contents pass through the sifting pan into the sluice pan. Now take both pans out of the water and remove the sifting pan. Do you see any big gold nuggets in there? No? OK—throw away the contents of the sifting pan. See image **a**.

5 The sluice pan should now be about a quarter full of material and even more full of water. Tilt the pan toward the gravity-trap riffles and move it side to side to wash the dirt off of the largest pebbles. Once the pebbles are clean, and you're sure none of them are gold nuggets, you can pick them out and toss them. See image **b**.

6 Now fill the sluice pan with water and transfer all of the contents to either the 14-inch or 10½-inch gravity pan, whichever one you're most comfortable with. See image **c**.

7 OK—here's where it gets interesting. Again hold the pan with the riffles on the downward side and tilt it so that you're cupping the sand and gravel in a crescent formed by the pan's bottom edge and sidewall. Now agitate the material by moving the pan from side to side. Because gold is heavier than gravel and sand, it will drop to the crease in the pan where the bottom meets the sidewall. As the gold sinks into the deepest part of the

pan, dip the front lip into the water and pull the pan back and slightly up. This will peel the top layer of gravel off while the gold remains safely underneath. See image **d**.

8 Repeat this process, shaking the pan from side to side to sink the gold and then dipping the front lip to peel away the top layer of gravel. Let gravity and water do the work. Remove any gold nuggets with your tweezers and place them in your vial. Once you've removed most of the sand, switch to the smooth side of the pan and continue the process, but shake more gently than before until only the gold remains. See images **e**, **f**, and **g**.

9 Suck up the gold flakes with your snuffer bottle. If there's still a little sand mixed in, don't worry. You can sift through it at home.

10 That's it! Go home and open your own Federal Reserve!

Where to Pan

PORTABLE PVC FISHING GEAR

Imagine being able to fish on a backpacking trip without having to tote an ungainly fishing pole and tackle box. Imagine having a setup so compact that you barely notice it in your backpack. Not only is this fantasy rig a real possibility, but you can make it yourself. Here's how.

DIFFICULTY LEVEL:
Car Camper

MATERIALS:

¾-inch MIP PVC plug

1-inch-diameter schedule 40 PVC pipe (12-inch piece)

1-inch-diameter PVC cap

18 inches black parachute cord

1 roll athletic tape

80 feet 3- to 10-pound-test fishing line

2 thick 1-inch-diameter rubber bands

3 of your favorite fishing lures

6 size-10 fishing hooks

8 size-5 split-shot weights

TOOLS:

Black spray paint (optional)

Hacksaw

Drill with ¼-inch bit

INSTRUCTIONS:

1 If you'd like to have a stealthy black fishing pole, paint all of the PVC parts now. Let them dry near a heat source for an hour, or overnight at room temperature.

2 Insert the ¾-inch MIP PVC plug into one end of the PVC pipe. See image **a**.

3 Cut a ½-inch-long slit into one side of the cap. Make the slit twice as wide as the saw blade is thick. See image **b**.

4 Drill a ¼-inch hole through the top of the cap. See image **c**.

5 Tie the ends of the para cord in an overhand knot and thread the other end of the resulting loop through the hole in the cap. See image **d**.

6 At the open end, cut a ½-inch-long slit into the side of the pipe.

7 Put the cap on the pipe. Starting ¼ inch from the base of the cap, wrap 4 inches of pipe with athletic tape. See image **e**.

8 Cut a ¹⁄₁₆-inch-deep groove across the pipe 4 inches from the plugged end. Do not cut through to the inside of the pipe. See image **f**.

9 Tie a clinch knot into the end of the fishing line. (To tie this knot, pass the line around pipe, make a few wraps around the standing part of the line, and then pass the end of the line between the wraps and the pipe.) Make sure the line rests in the slit, and pull the knot tight. See image **g**.

10 Pull the fishing line toward the plugged end and wrap a 3-inch piece of tape around the pipe to cover the knot. This will not only hold the knot in place but also ensure that the line doesn't snag on the knot when cast. See image **h**.

11 Wrap about 80 feet of fishing line around this piece of tape. Don't cut the line yet. Just cover the wraps with the rubber band to hold them in place.

12 Using a clinch knot, tie your favorite lure to the end of the line. As a kid, I had lots of luck using a Luhr-Jensen Super Duper, so that's what I attached.

a b c d e

13 The inside of the tube is now your tackle box. Fill it with extra hooks, split shot, lures, and bobbers. You can even put a pocketknife in there. There's plenty of room. See image **i**.

14 Put your newly tied lure into the pipe as well. Capture the fishing line in the gap formed by the slits in the cap and pipe. This gap will prevent the line from getting kinked and weakened. See image **j**.

15 Now you have a highly portable rod and tackle box. Toss it in your backpack, or even in your back pocket, and hike to your favorite alpine lake. See image **k**.

16 Here's how to use it: Take off the cap and pull out the tied lure. Replace the cap and remove the rubber band.

17 Pull 3 feet of line off the spool and hold the rest of it on with your thumb. Swing the lure over your head in a counterclockwise motion. When you've got it swinging as fast as you can, whip the lure toward the water and take your thumb off the spool.

18 Slowly wrap the line around the pipe to reel it in. When you feel the fish bite, give the line a quick jerk to set the hook and reel it in!

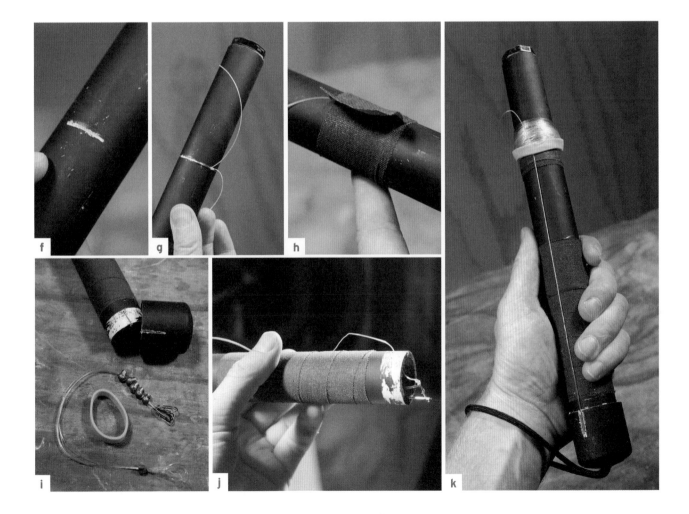

DAISY-CHAIN HEADBAND

Imagine ancient times, when princesses (and princes) were crowned with flowers in their hair. Ah, to wear the best that nature has to offer while running barefoot through tall grass and letting your fingers trail over the sea of stalks. Yes, that is a peaceful, easy feeling, my friends. You don't need to be a hippie to appreciate a beautiful chain of flowers in your hair. Nature's beauty never goes out of style. Spread the love, man!

DIFFICULTY LEVEL:
Weekend Warrior

MATERIALS:

6 to 12 fresh-picked flowers with stems longer than 2 inches

Lovely person to adorn

INSTRUCTIONS:

1 Find a cluster of flowers, preferably not in your neighbor's front yard. See image **a**.

2 Pick about six flowers with stems that are all about the same length.

3 Grab your first flower and, about ½ inch up from the bottom of the stem, pinch the stalk lengthwise with your thumbnail. Push your thumbnail through to create a slit that's a little longer than the stem is wide. See images **b** and **c**.

4 Thread the stem of your next flower all the way through this slit, so that its blossom is snug against the stem of the first. See image **d**.

5 Now, making sure to keep ½ inch of solid stem below, make a slit in the second flower stem just like the first.

6 Keep going like this until your chain of flowers is about 12 inches long. See image **e**.

7 OK—it's time for the first fitting. Gently drape the flowers around your prince or princess's head to see if it fits. If it doesn't, add more flowers until it does.

8 Now make another slit in the stem of the very first flower just below the base of the blossom. Then gently, draping the middle of the chain across your subject's forehead, bring the two ends back to meet behind his or her head.

9 Insert the last flower's stem into the slit you just made. Give it a gentle tug—gentle is the watchword here—to tighten the chain so that it fits. See image **f**.

10 Great. Now remove the ring of flowers (gently, of course) and make one final slit in the stem of the first flower, midway down. Bend the stem of the last flower around and insert it into the new slit. That will keep everything together. See **Daisy Chain** illustration and image **g**.

11 Crown your prince, princess, duke, or damsel; break out your acoustic guitar; and get ready for some frolicking! See image **h**.

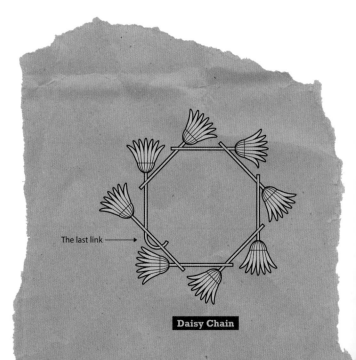

The last link

Daisy Chain

MAKE A BUNDLE BOW

Here's a worst-case-scenario: you're camping with a teenager and his iPad battery runs out.

Let's face it, without a constant stream of media, he's going to be antsy. Leaf rubbings may not do the trick. You need a project with more of an edge, or rather, a point. That's where this bundle bow comes in handy. You can find most of the materials around your campsite.

DIFFICULTY LEVEL:
Backwoodsman

MATERIALS:

3 straight branches as a tall as the archer

50 feet parachute cord

TOOLS:

Hatchet, or pocketknife with a locking blade

INSTRUCTIONS:

1 Find three straight 1- to 1½-inch-thick branches that are about as tall as the person you're making the bow for. Either green or dead branches will work. Often you can find the branches you need just lying on the ground. Barring that, saplings growing near a river or lake work well. See image **a**. Test them by bending them first. They should be stiff but not brittle. If they bend too easily or snap, they won't work for this project.

2 If you need to cut branches, a hatchet works best. See image **b**. If all you have is a pocketknife, though, you can use a log to hammer the tip of the blade into a branch to cut it free. *WARNING: Do this only if your knife has a locking blade. With a nonlocking blade, there's great risk of the blade snapping shut onto your fingers.*

3 The thickest of your branches will be the main branch. Trim it so that it stands as tall as the archer. Remember, throughout this project and whenever you're working with sharp tools, to always cut away from yourself.

4 Trim the next-thickest branch, starting at the narrow end, until it's two-thirds the length of your main branch. See image **c**.

5 Do the same with the narrowest branch, trimming it to half the length of the main branch. See image **d**.

6 Using your knife or hatchet, cut off all of the twigs and burrs so the three branches are as smooth as possible. See images **e** and **f**.

7 Make a small mark with your knife at the midpoint of each branch. See image **g**.

8 Cut your para cord into eight 5-foot-long pieces, double up one end of each piece, and tie an overhand knot to make a loop. Set these aside for the moment. See image **h**.

9 Place the two largest branches so that their thick ends are opposite each other and their midpoints meet. Now rotate the branches so that they fit together as snugly as possible. See images **i** and **j**.

10 Hold the two branches together and make another mark across them with your knife. This mark will make it easy to find the branches' "best fit" orientation if they get separated.

11 Now add the smallest branch to the bundle, lining up the midpoints and making sure its thick end is on the same side of the midpoint as the main branch's thick end. Rotate the small branch until it lies as snugly as possible against the other two.

12 Make another cut across all three branches to mark their proper orientation in case they get separated.

13 Grab one of the pieces of para cord from Step 8 and make a loop around the bundle about 3 or 4 inches below the midpoint. To do this, just wrap the cord once around the bundle, thread the end of the cord through the figure-eight loop, and pull it tight. See image **j** and **Assembling the Bundle Bow** illustration.

14 Pull the cord tight and wrap it around the bundle four or five times, laying each successive wrap snugly against the previous one, until you have 1 foot of cord left.

g

h

i

j

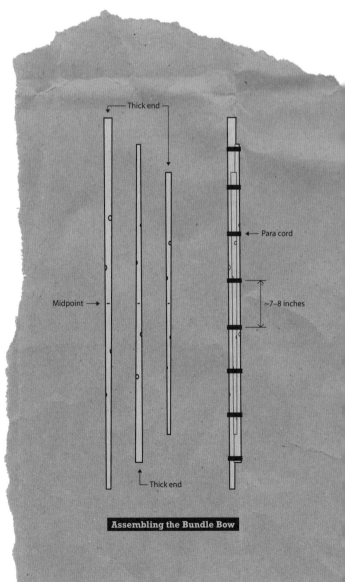

Thick end

Para cord

Midpoint →

~7–8 inches

Thick end

Assembling the Bundle Bow

15 Make a bight in the cord and thread it under the wraps at the biggest gap between the branches. See image **k**.

16 Pull the end of the cord through the bight to make a half hitch. See image **l**.

17 Tie four or five more successive half hitches and finish with one big half hitch around all the wraps. Trim off any remaining cord, leaving about an inch. These wrapped knots, which we'll space 7 to 8 inches apart, will hold the bow together. Let's do a few more. See images **m** and **n**.

18 Grab another piece of para cord, squeeze the branches tightly together, and make the same wrapped knot as before, 3 or 4 inches above the bow's midpoint.

19 Make another wrapped knot, capturing all three branches, 2 inches from the end of the shortest branch. Before you thread the first loop, though, carve a notch in the branches to hold the cord so that it won't slip when the bow is under tension. Now do this again 2 inches from the other end of the shortest branch. See image **o**.

20 Make another wrapped knot a couple of inches from each end of the middle-length branch, carving a notch for each first loop.

21 Now look at the bow. Is there a gap between any of the knots that's greater than 7 or 8 inches? If so, split the difference and tie a wrapped knot there.

22 To complete the bow, let's make a couple of notches to hold the bowstring. Notice that the three branches have a slight curve. This indicates the direction in which the bow will naturally bend. Cut the notches ¼ inch deep into the main branch, on the outside of the curve, about 2 inches from both the top and bottom of the bow. They should angle down toward where your hand will be when you draw the bow. See image **p** for more detail.

23 Cut a piece of para cord about 6 feet long and tie a figure-eight loop in both ends. The distance between the loops should be about five-sixths the length of the bow.

24 Put one loop around the bottom of the bow, laid into the notch you just carved. Now place the end of the bow on the ground and pull the other loop up to eye level. Keep the cord taut!

25 Now, with the bottom of the bow firmly planted at your feet, place the inside curve against the back of your leg (your left leg, if you're right-handed) and bend the top of the bow down to meet the loop. You may have to adjust the loop, if the cord is too tight or loose. To check, make a "thumbs-up" sign with your hand by placing the bottom of your fist against the inside of the bow at its midpoint. On a properly strung bow your thumb will just touch the bowstring. See images **q** and **r**.

26 Pull back the bowstring and prepare to be amazed by its power! See image **s**.

27 Now all you need are some arrows. Find some straight, 4-foot-long, ¾-inch-thick branches and trim them down with your knife or hatchet to make them as smooth as possible. Pay extra attention to cleaning up the base of the arrow to make its shaft straight and its back end flat.

28 Carve a point into the forward end of the arrow. If you want to go the extra mile, heat the arrows in the fire (without charring them) to make them stiffer. See image **t**.

29 The last step is to cut notches into the backs of the arrows. First, though, we have to see how the arrows lie. Hold the tip of one between your thumb and index finger and the back end as if you were going to shoot it. As you loosen your grip on the back end, the arrow may want to roll or "relax." After it does, note the arrow's orientation and mark an up-and-down line on its back end. Place your blade on this line and carve a notch about ¼ inch wide and just as deep. Use the edge of the blade, though, not the tip. Using the tip will split the wood. Repeat this for all of your arrows. See images **u** and **v**.

30 You're done! Take the arrows out and see how they fly!

COMPASS TREASURE HUNT

When was the last time your kids heard this call to action? "Avast, ye scurvy dogs! Take this treasure map and find the booty me and me mates buried on this here bloomin' island." The best part is that, while your kids are out frantically searching for a veritable treasure trove of chocolate coins and Jolly Ranchers, they'll be using a compass to learn valuable orienteering skills. And, if all goes according to plan, they'll be amped up and crashed out by bedtime.

DIFFICULTY LEVEL:
Weekend Warrior

MATERIALS:

Compass (Silva, Suunto, and Brunton all make quality compasses.)

Pen and paper

Matches or lighter (optional)

Coffee or tea (optional)

Gold chocolate coins and/or hard candy

INSTRUCTIONS:

1 Standing at a specific point within your campsite or yard, look around for a clearly visible tree or rock about 100 feet away.

2 Holding the compass at chest level, point the direction-of-travel arrows at your target. See **How to Use a Compass** on page 110.

3 Align the "N" (north) on the outer dial with the red end of the compass needle.

4 Read the bearing on the outer ring at the point indicated on the illustration.

5 Walk toward the object, counting off the number of paces it takes you to get there. Remember that the length of your stride may be longer than your kids', so try to adjust your steps to a kid's stride to give accurate directions.

6 Now write a pirate-themed note stating the bearing and distance (the number of paces) to the nearby treasure, such as 60° and 42 paces. For added authenticity, burn the edges and stain the paper with coffee or tea.

7 Stash these treasure coordinates to hand off to your treasure hunters later.

8 Place gold coins or candy at the first waypoint. Be sure these are visible enough so that your kids know they're on the right track.

9 From your first waypoint, site another object and write down the coordinates, as in Steps 2 through 5. Leave the directions to the second waypoint at the first site, so that your kids can follow the trail.

10 Leave some treasure at this second site as well.

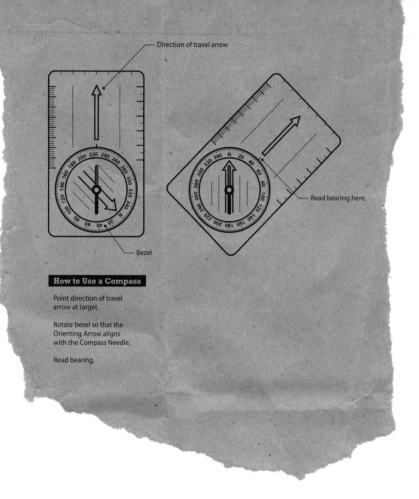

Direction of travel arrow

Read bearing here.

Bezel

How to Use a Compass

Point direction of travel
arrow at target.

Rotate bezel so that the
Orienting Arrow aligns
with the Compass Needle.

Read bearing.

⓫ Repeat this as many times as you like. I like to have one treasure site for every kid in the search party.

⓬ Be sure to set your campsite or house as the final waypoint. (Hint: If you plot the course in reverse, you won't have to backtrack to leave the instructions to the next waypoint after you pace out the distance. Just remember to face the other way to get the bearing; otherwise you'll send your kids off in the opposite direction.)

⓭ Now it's time to gather your pint-size pirates and tell them that the hills are brimming with treasure. Let them also know that in order to find this treasure, they'll have to learn a valuable and important skill, one that might save their lives one day.

⓮ Instruct them in the use of the compass, i.e., Steps 2 through 4 (sighting a target, aligning north on the outer ring to the needle, and reading the bearing).

⓯ Have each kid, one at a time, sight an object in the distance and give you its bearing.

⓰ Now, in your best Blackbeard voice, request a volunteer to start off the expedition, and hand him or her the compass and the map to the first waypoint.

⓱ Don't fail to mention that there's a curse for those who plunder more than one treasure for themselves. Every member of the crew should take a turn at the compass and track down his or her own treasure.

⓲ While they're away, set up a feast for the treasure hunters' triumphant return. Good times will be had by all!

Note: Also show your kids that the compass works similarly with a map. Just place the edge of the compass on the imaginary line between where you are and where you're going, turn the bezel so north on the compass lines up with north on the map, and read the bearing as before.

AAARGH...
SHIVER ME TIMBERS!
YE PLUNDERED ALL
ME PIRATE LOOT!

SCALLYWAGS, I'LL SEE YOU
IN DAVEY JONES LOCKER!

310° @ 120 PACES :)

TARP SURFING

When the swell is way too gnarly at your favorite beach break, you can grab your four-wheeled stick and make your own sick surf spot. That's right—I'm talking about tarp surfing. It's always goin' off; the conditions are always glassy; and your kids will want to spend all day getting tubed. Be sure to bring your camera to capture the epic action.

DIFFICULTY LEVEL:
Backwoodsman

MATERIALS:

Large broom with firm bristles

For longer waves, one 30-by-60-foot blue poly tarp (This size is my choice!)

For bigger barrels, one 40-by-50-foot blue poly tarp

Two 4-foot pieces parachute cord

Two 5-inch sections garden hose or PVC pipe

Three 30-pound, rubber-ended dumbbells

Four 5-pound, rubber-coated free weights

Longboard-style skateboard with street wheels

Camera with a wide-angle lens (optional)

Spotlights (optional)

FASTENERS:

One roll of heavy-duty duct tape

TOOLS:

6-foot ladder (optional)

INSTRUCTIONS:

1 Just as in the world of big-wave surfing, sweet tarp-surfing spots aren't a dime a dozen. Look for a big flat paved area (a freshly paved street, parking lot, or cul-de-sac) and sweep the area clear of any debris.

2 In each corner of the tarp, make an 18-by-8-inch patch of duct tape, offset 1 inch in from the edges. Do this for both sides. See image **a**.

3 Thread a piece of para cord through each of the 5-inch pieces of hose to form handles. Tie one to the corner of the tarp where you'll start your pull. We'll call that Corner A. (Imagine a large, vertical rectangle. We'll name the corners in a clockwise direction starting with Corner A in the upper left. See **Tarp Surfing** illustration. Save your other handle for later. See images **b** and **c**.

4 Set one 30-pound dumbbell onto each of the remaining taped corners and pull the tarp tight to eliminate any wrinkles. A tug on each corner should do the trick. Place the weight at Corner B so that the tarp can pull free as the wave gets bigger. See image **d**.

5 Space the 5-pound free weights evenly on the long side of the tarp opposite Corner A (the side between corners B and C). You should have a weight every 12 feet or so.

6 Alright—it's time to check your break. Grab your handle at Corner A and, in one motion, pull it up over your head and walk toward the midpoint between corners B and C. Did you get a sweet curl? Nice work, brah! See image **e**.

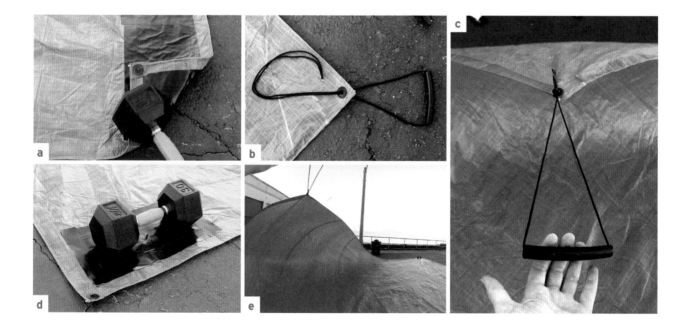

7 Adjust any weights that may have moved during your test run and make sure that the tarp is flat to reduce the risk of wipeouts. As you pull the tarp for the next break, have your surfer skate diagonally across the tarp from Corner B to Corner D.

8 Pull the tarp tight between each break. If you rip any portion of the tarp, repair both sides with duct tape. For big tears, duct-tape in a new piece of tarp as a patch.

9 Switch it up and don't snake the waves! Let some-one that was on corner-pulling duty rotate in. And don't forget to position a photographer in the surf to capture the action. That's called the Picture Perfect Barrel. But this is a versatile break—there are other types waves you can generate. See image **f**.

10 If you swap the remaining handle for the dumbbell at Corner B and move the free weights to the tarp edge between corners C and D, you'll get the Close Out. Have your surfer start from the middle between the two handles while your surf handlers pull the wave straight down toward the line of free weights. At the end of the run, the surfer will get buried under mounds of tarp.

11 If you attach your handles at Corners A and D, you'll get the Long Hollow Tube. Just put a dumbbell at Corners B and C, and one at the midpoint between the two. Space the free weights evenly along that same edge. Have your surfer start near Corner A and head to the opposite edge while your wave handlers pull their corners straight across toward the row of weights. The handler at Corner A should start a second earlier than the one at Corner D. Have your surfer see if they can make it all the way across the wave before getting pummeled in the surf.

12 For night surfing, place a couple of spotlights behind the wave and see what kinds of rad shots you can get. Lie in the surf and aim the camera down the pipeline! Shoot overhead from a ladder! *Pavement Surfer* Magazine will never believe the photos!

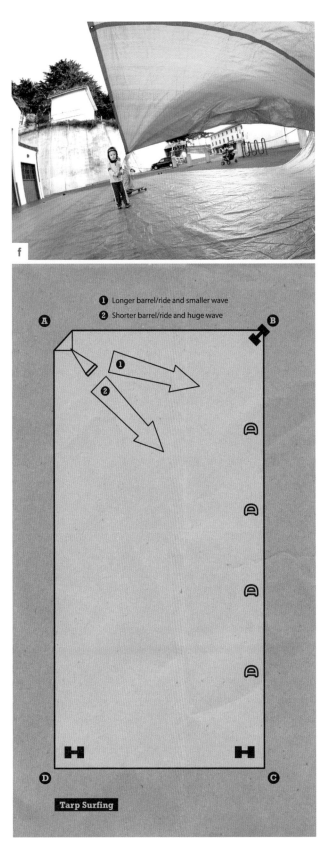

f

1 Longer barrel/ride and smaller wave
2 Shorter barrel/ride and huge wave

Tarp Surfing

LEAF RUBBINGS

When fall arrives and leaves lie scattered on the ground, your thoughts may turn to raking. And I'll bet your children's thoughts turn to jumping into the fresh leaf piles you've just raked. Such is life. But before those leaves fade away for the year, why not show your kids how to turn nature's castoffs into works of art? A journal full of rubbed leaves lasts all season and is a good way for a budding biologist to document her finds. Record the date and location and try to identify the tree! Or go free-form and have your young earth artist decorate a tree that you paint in the corner of his room.

DIFFICULTY LEVEL:
Weekend Warrior

MATERIALS:

Leaves of various shapes and sizes (Choose ones that aren't too dry and brown.)

5 to 10 sheets letter-size printer paper (Not card or cover stock—it's too thick.)

Jumbo-size crayons with the paper peeled off

Pencil or pen

Double-sided mini tape (tape that's about one-third the width of standard Scotch tape)

INSTRUCTIONS:

1 Go out and search for a variety of leaves that you find beautiful or interesting. Make sure they're still pretty green. Brown ones will crumble. See image **a**.

2 Select a leaf to start with and place it vertically, on a hard surface, with the vein side facing up. See image **b**.

3 Place a blank sheet of paper over the leaf, covering it entirely, and grab a crayon. See image **c**.

4 With one hand, place your thumb on the paper over the stem, and your index or middle finger on the paper over the top of the leaf, to hold it in place. Be sure not to let the paper or the leaf move as you rub or you'll get a double image. More on that later.

5 Hold the crayon, sideways, over the area of the paper that is covering the leaf.

6 Are you ready? OK. Firmly rub the crayon all over the leaf and watch the image magically appear. See image **d**.

7 Take the flat end of the crayon and rub it down on the paper in between the major veins of the leaf to bring out details that the first pass didn't reveal.

8 Now, using the pointed end of the crayon, gently work the remaining unfilled areas to bring out even more detail. Be careful not to tear the paper.

9 Write down the date and location of your leaf find. Have your kids identified the type of leaf? Nice work! Write that down, too.

10 Now you can cut out the leaf, and its description, so your kids can tape it to the tree painting in their room or into a journal. Either way, use the double-sided tape for this. They can also save a step by rubbing the leaves directly into their journals. See image **e**.

11 If you're feeling artistic, try two colors for the same leaf, for example, green on the outer edges and yellow on the inside. Try moving the leaf during the rubbing to create overlapping shapes, or switch to a new leaf entirely. How many rubbings can you fit on a page to create a composition? In leaf rubbing, as in life, the possibilities are endless.

CATCH LIZARDS

The lizard, with its speed, agility, and abundance in the wild, makes a fine introduction to the world of reptiles. Catch one and you've got your hands on 200 million years of evolution in a 4-inch package. Here's how to catch them.

Note: Be gentle with this noose so no lizards will be harmed.

DIFFICULTY LEVEL:
Weekend Warrior

INSTRUCTIONS:

1 Grab a long blade of wild grass and tear the seeds off of the end. Tie the thin end of the grass into a slipknot, leaving an inch of grass beyond the knot itself. See **Lizard Noose** illustration and images **a** and **b**.

2 Find a lizard. They usually hang out on sunny rocks or logs. Approach slowly from behind or from the side. If you stay 3 or 4 feet away, they shouldn't run. Reach out and place the noose around the lizard's neck. The lizard, more concerned with your proximity, won't see the noose coming. Give the blade of grass a quick tug and—bam!

3 Grab the lizard and gently but quickly turn him over onto his back. Check out his belly! Rub it (again, be gentle) and he'll fall into a dreamy, relaxed state.

4 Now delicately remove the noose. Be sure not to grab the lizard by the tail, though. It may come off. Even though lizards can shed their tails to fool predators, they are more vulnerable without them.

5 If you stop rubbing your lizard, he'll wake up, but slowly enough that he can be observed, studied, or placed on a sleeping sister.

MATERIALS:

2- to 4-foot blade wild grass

Lizard Noose

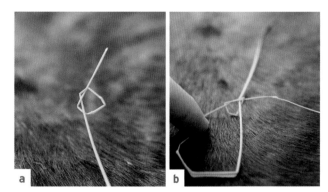

a   b

DISC GOLF

Golf is fun and all, but carrying your clubs on a backpacking trip can be a real drag. And besides, after you set up camp, where are you going to play? You could build your own course, but by the time you finish smoothing out the green on the first hole, your trip will be over. Believe me, I've tried. Thankfully there's a simple solution to all of this backbreaking labor—it's disc golf. You can tee up, putt, and birdie to your heart's content on a course you design yourself, no raking needed.

If you want to kick it up a notch, grab some flashlights and glow-in-the-dark Frisbees, and head out for a night game of "Tron Golf." What's up now, Master Control?

Having a dedicated set of discs specially designed for the varied throws the game requires is a luxury. That said, it makes for better game play. Here's the lowdown on three disc types. All can be thrown with the normal backhand style, the two-fingered forehand style, or the overhead tomahawk throw.

DIFFICULTY LEVEL:
Car Camper

MATERIALS:

Some regular Frisbees that your dog hasn't yet chewed up, or . . . three disc-golf flying discs per person: a driver, an approach disc, and a putter

Scorecard

Pencils

Markers

THE BASIC DISC

A basic 110 to 175 gram disc is fine for your disc golf if you don't want to get too fancy.

THE DRIVER

This disc is made for distance. It has a sharp edge, which can be hard to control, but it can fly fast and far if it's thrown right. The key is to hold it about head height and give it a good, fast spin on release.

THE APPROACH DISC

This disc has a soft rubber feel, as opposed to the hard, plastic feel of the driver. It is easier to control but also doesn't fly as far.

THE PUTTER

This disc is the softest of the group—it's almost squishy. It flies slow, has a blunt edge, and is very easy to throw and control.

Note: Disc-golf equipment may not yet have made it to your local sporting-goods store, but you can find plenty of suppliers online.

INSTRUCTIONS:

1 Grab your discs and gather at the first tee. You're still at your campsite? Perfect—that's where the first tee is.

2 Pick an object about 100 yards away and designate it as Hole 1. In picking 9 or 18 holes, be sure to add some variety. The elevation can go up or down; discs can fly over obstacles like lakes or streams; they can fly through challenging terrain like rocky outcrops or a stand of trees. One thing to remember: In disk golf, every hole is par 3, so pick your distances accordingly.

3 Have you agreed on Hole 1? Can everyone see it? OK—you're ready for the first drive. Draw a line in the ground to represent the tee. Have the first player take as many steps as they need when throwing the first drive, but make sure they don't cross the line. If they do, mark them down for one stroke and have them throw again. The best drives fly straight and true, 6 to 10 feet off the ground. Have all the other players throw, as well. See image **a**.

4 Now have each player find his or her disc and leave a marker to identify the spot. The person farthest from the hole throws first. The same rules apply as before. Take as many steps as you like when you throw, but don't step past the marker.

5 Keep playing like this until your group is within about 100 feet of the first hole. Now it's time to use the approach discs. When you find yourself within 50 feet, break out the putters. Let's say your first hole is a tree. Hitting it with the disc anywhere between knee height and 8 feet up counts as a score. If you can't see the trunk, hitting the branches is fine. If it's a rock, anywhere on the rock is fine. Here the rules change a bit. The players need to keep their feet planted behind the marker, no steps this time. If they fall forward or step past the marker, it's another stroke on the scorecard and a do-over.

6 Alright! Where's the next hole? On the other side of the gorge? Across the little alpine lake? Or to the top of the far boulder? It's wherever you decide. The player that completes the course with the fewest throws wins. Keep track of your score so the loser knows whose job it is to supply the Otter Pops or cold brewskis, whichever the case may be.

Fore! If you see any raccoons, ask if they mind if you play through.

GEOCACHE

Did you know that a secret world of hidden treasures exists right under your nose? What's more, this treasure trove spans the globe. How can you get your hands on these secret stashes, you ask?

Well, first of all, they're called caches, geocaches to be precise (and you'll need to be precise!). Your guide to these amazing finds is a GPS device or smart phone, and a cache list, which can be found on any of several geocaching sites. I recommend the largest, www.geocaching.com. The process isn't all plunder and pillage, though. If you take something from a cache, geocaching protocol requires you leave something of greater value in its place.

DIFFICULTY LEVEL:
Car Camper

MATERIALS:

A treasure of your own, to leave in the geocache you find (Something small—like a plastic animal figurine, a Matchbox car, or a pair of dice—is perfect.)

TOOLS:

Groundspeak geocaching app for iPhone or Android phone, or any Global Positioning System (GPS) device (You'll need one or the other.)

Computer or laptop

INSTRUCTIONS:

1 Pick your favorite online geocaching site. I recommend Geocaching.com. Log on and create an account.

2 Download the Groundspeak app for your iPhone or Android phone.

3 Now you can choose to find a cache or to hide one. I recommend finding a few first to get a better idea of how things work.

4 Open the Groundspeak app on your phone and select "Find Nearby Caches." The app will automatically display the geocaches closest to you.

5 Select a cache from the list on your preferred site and check its difficulty rating. On www.geocaching.com, caches with a one-star rating are easy to find, while caches with a five-star rating are nearly impossible. Start with the easiest ones and work your way up to the tough stuff.

6 Take a look at the terrain rating, too. Again, one star is easy; five stars is hard.

7 How big or small is it? The bar with the little boxes shows the cache's size, which can vary from the size of a pea to the size of a large shoebox. Assess these factors and decide if the cache is one you'd like to pursue.

8 Also listed on this summary page (if you bought the paid app) are the cache's GPS coordinates, which will get you pretty close without revealing the exact location.

9 Now select "Description" and read the notes. These will describe what the cache looks like, the approximate size, and possibly some clues to help find it.

10 Now you're ready for the hunt! Select the "Let's Go!" icon (iPhone) or "Navigate to Geocache" (Android). Select "Map" and you will see your location represented by a blue dot and the cache represented by a green icon.

11 If you choose to use your phone's compass, remember that, unlike a regular compass, the red pointer will point toward the geocache. Once you're close, use this to find the most direct route.

12 Let's start with the map. Head toward the green icon. If you need help along the way, back up one screen and use the directions or the compass.

13 Using these built-in navigation aids and the details on the summary page, you'll be able to get pretty close to the cache. If you have a GPS device that can give you your exact latitude and longitude, you can get within 15 feet. If you need it, and if the option is available, select "Hints" to get detailed clues as to the cache's location. Keep in mind, though, depending on the difficulty of the cache, the clue may be more misleading than helpful.

14 If you find the cache and take something from it, be sure to place something of greater value in its place. Also don't forget to log into the logbook to document that you found the cache. With a premium membership to www.geocaching.com, you can upload your photos and write about your experience to share with others.

15 Are you getting pretty good at this? Alright—I've got a challenge for you. To find a cache I recently placed, look up "Double Red Nest" in San Francisco. It's a small cache placed on 1/26/2011 with the following coordinates:

N 37° 46.178'   W 122° 26.471'

The difficulty rating is four stars, and the terrain rating is four! Good luck!

16 Now, if you'd like to hide your own cache, log into your www.geocaching.com account and click "Hide & Seek a Cache." Then follow the instructions under "Hide a Cache."

A recent geocaching trek took me to the end of a public dock and what appeared to be a locked gate. Yet when I checked it, it was open. I walked down the dock. On my upgraded version of Groundspeak, I could see by the coordinates that I was within inches of the cache, but still no luck. Sitting on the dock was an aloe plant whose pot was filled with figurines, plastic animals, and toys. Could it be in there? It wasn't. Then I remembered a hint I had read: "The captain gives you permission to come aboard." Hanging on a rope that blocked access to a lower dock was a sign that read, "Boarding by permission of captain only."

A-ha! I unhooked the rope, walked down to the lower dock, and doubled back to my original coordinates. I was exactly under the aloe plant. Bam—there it was! Mounted underneath the dock was a water-bottle holder, the kind you might see on a mountain bike. It held a plastic bottle, the geocache.

I opened it up, found the sign-in card, and wrote down my username, Thrash Gordon, along with the date. I didn't take any of the treasure (a little plastic frog, a photo, a plastic jewel, and an interesting-looking stone) but left a wing-suiting sticker. (Wing suiting is one of my other hobbies!) I tucked the bottle back in place and headed off to find another cache.

Success!

SLACKLINE

What's slacklining, you ask? Imagine tightrope walking on a single strand of nylon webbing and you've got it. Sure, some people go extreme and bounce on a slackline stretched across a gorge, but your kids can start mild-style by stretching a line between two trees. It's a great way for them to work on balance, challenge a fear of heights, and have some fun. And since they'll only be three or four feet off the ground, no safety lines are required.

DIFFICULTY LEVEL:
Backwoodsman

MATERIALS:

Two 12-foot pieces 1-inch tubular webbing to use as anchoring slings

Two 12-by-36-inch carpet pieces

60 to 80 feet 2-inch tubular webbing (Some slackliners prefer flat webbing over tubular because it cinches better under a load, but at a load rating of 7,500 pounds, both are plenty strong.)

4 carabiners rated for 30 kilonewtons or a 7,500-pound load

INSTRUCTIONS:

1 Start by finding two trees 8 inches or greater in diameter between which to rig the slackline. Ideally, the trees should be 40 to 60 feet apart and separated by a grassy area that's free of exposed roots or rocks.

2 Grab one of your lengths of 1-inch webbing and tie the ends together with a water knot. (A water knot is basically two overhand knots inside one another.) To tie one, simply tie an overhand knot into one end of the webbing, then feed the other end of the webbing through the knot, in the opposite direction, tracing it loop for loop. Now tighten. You should have one tail end of the webbing on each side of the knot when you're done. See **Water Knot** illustration. Do this with the other piece of webbing, as well. See images **a**, **b**, and **c**. These will be the anchoring slings.

3 Wrap the first tree with carpet at a point about 4 feet off the ground. Keep the soft carpet side facing outward to protect the slings. Carry the other piece of carpet to the base of the second tree. See image **d**.

4 Wrap your sling around the tree (twice if possible) and link the ends together with a carabiner. To make things easier, hook the other three carabiners and the other sling to a belt loop or pants pocket. See image **e**.

5 Tie a Munter hitch around the carabiner with one end of the 2-inch webbing and back it up with a slipped half hitch. See **Munter Hitch Locked with a Slipped Half Hitch** illustration. To see the knot in action, check out images **f** through **k**.

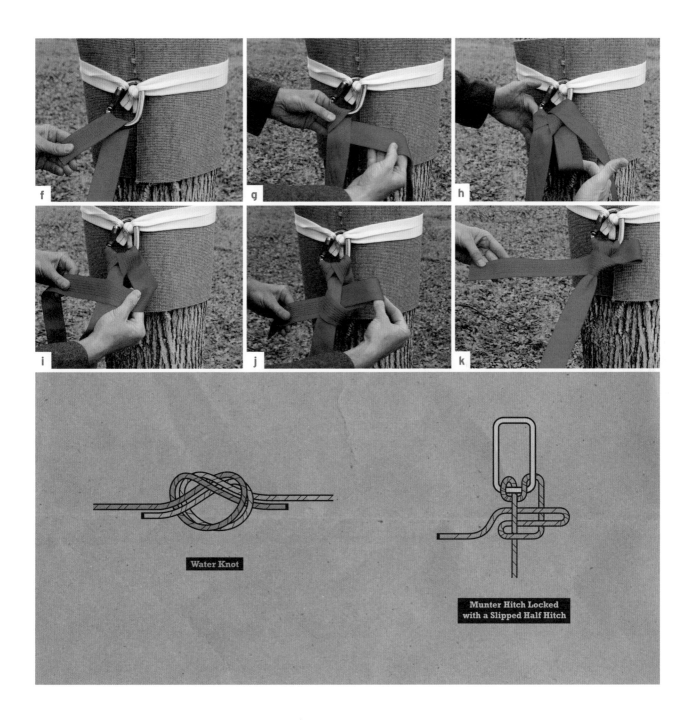

Water Knot

Munter Hitch Locked
with a Slipped Half Hitch

6 Pull the 2-inch webbing to within 10 feet of the second tree. Stop, grab a carabiner, pull a loop of webbing through it, then fold the loop over the carabiner to form a lanyard hitch. See photos. Let's call this your "pulley" carabiner. Be sure to keep the webbing taut throughout this step to keep the sling from sliding down the first tree. See images **l**, **m**, **n** and **o**.

7 Leave the carabiner there and continue toward the second tree. Step on the end of the 2-inch webbing to keep it taut, and wrap the carpet and sling around the second tree as you did with the first. This time, however, connect the ends of the sling with two carabiners.

8 Now we're going to rig a tackle with the 2-inch webbing (a tension knot) to cinch it tight. First run the webbing down through the top carabiner, then over to and down through the PULLEY carabiner, then back to the bottom carabiner, pulling the webbing up through it from bottom to top (opposite to the direction in which you passed the webbing through the top carabiner). See **Tension Knot** illustration and images **p**, **q**, and **r**.

9 Now take another pass back through the PULLEY carabiner. Thread the webbing down through the top as before, but this time passing it inside the loop that's already there. Check image **s** to see what I mean.

10 Now pull the tail end of the webbing as hard as you can. The tackle will form a friction lock to hold the slackline taut. Pull until you can't pull anymore. See image **t**.

11 Tie the remaining 2-inch webbing with a slipped half hitch. Make a long loop forming the slipped part of the hitch and tie that off in another half hitch. See images **u** through **y**.

12 Have your slackliners get on and give it a try. Here are some tips: The slackline moves around less the closer you are to the trees, so try starting there. Also, don't look at the slackline, or your feet. Just focus on a point on the opposite tree and get in the zone.

13 Do you feel yourself becoming steadier? Try sitting Indian-style, or break out a horizontal handstand. You're on your way to becoming a master!

14 To loosen the friction knot when you're done, undo the half hitches and pull the tail of the webbing sideways, away from the carabiner.

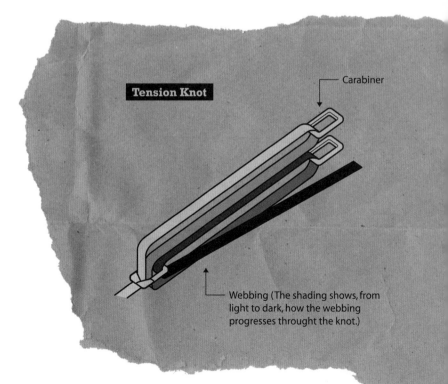

Tension Knot

Carabiner

Webbing (The shading shows, from light to dark, how the webbing progresses throught the knot.)

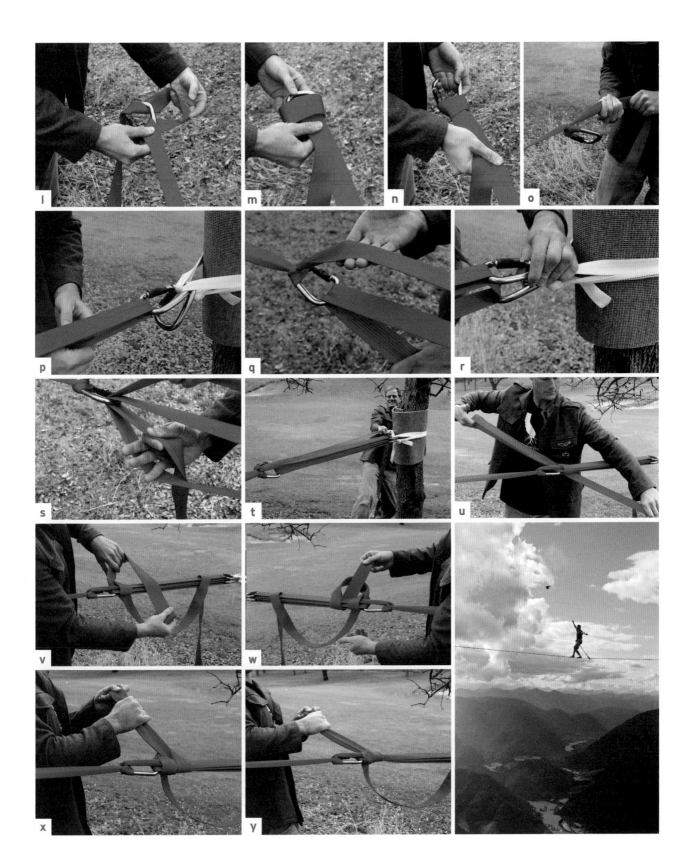

FLASHLIGHT TAG

Do you remember playing flashlight tag as a kid? The running around, the heart-pumping adrenaline of trying to be so quiet while others were on the prowl—those are the joys of summer. If your kids don't know about this game, do them a favor and let them in on the fun.

DIFFICULTY LEVEL:
Weekend Warrior

MATERIALS:

1 or 2 large flashlights (depending on the number of players)

INSTRUCTIONS:

1 First establish a perimeter for the playing field. Fifty square yards or so should do. Make sure everyone knows the boundaries, because the game becomes unplayable if kids wander off.

2 Designate the "jail" area where kids go once they're tagged—a large boulder or tree works well.

3 Choose one person to be "it." Give this person the flashlight and let them know that the light should stay on at all times; no covering or blocking the beam.

4 Now have the seeker count down, aloud, from 30. The countdown is everyone else's signal to disappear. If they can't find a hiding spot, they can move around.

5 Now the search begins. To tag someone, the seeker must shine the light on the hider and call out their name and their hiding spot. If the seeker correctly identifies the hider, the hider goes to jail. If the seeker misidentifies the hider, the hider identifies himself and the seeker must cover his or her eyes and count down from 30 again while the hider finds a new hiding place.

6 Was someone tagged? Oops, they go to jail (to sit on the boulder or touch the tree) to wait until the start of the next round.

7 Those in the clink can be tagged and set free by players still in the game. If they can do so without getting caught themselves, that is!

8 After all of the mayhem, the last person caught becomes "it" for the next round.

9 If there are more than six or seven players, try having two people be "it" at once. Now team strategy comes into play.

BUILD A BRIDGE ACROSS A STREAM

What do you do when you can't cross a stream? Turn around? No! Put on your civil engineering hat and build a bridge!

DIFFICULTY LEVEL:
Backwoodsman

MATERIALS:

6 -to 12-foot-long fallen log, with a 6- to 10-inch diameter

4 to 6 large rocks

TOOLS:

Shovel (optional)

INSTRUCTIONS:

1 Scout out a good log first, then find the closest viable spot to bridge the stream—that way, you'll keep the log-dragging portion of this project to a minimum. See image **a**.

2 Next, find four of the biggest rocks you can carry and place them next to your bridge site.

3 The first goal is to place two rocks at the water's edge, 2 inches closer together than the log is wide. They should also be able to support the bottom of the log at least 12 inches above the water. Before you place them, though, dig or form an indentation for the boulders to sit in—that way they won't move around when you stand on them. These will be your foundation stones. See image **b**.

4 Now stack another rock or two on top of the first ones to form a fulcrum on which to pivot the log. Make sure the rocks are solidly stacked.

5 Drag the log over to your bridge site. One way to do this is to lay smaller logs along your path, almost like railroad ties, and drag the log across them. This will make it much easier to move the log.

6 Lift the wider end of the log onto your fulcrum stones (bend from the knees!). Keep going until you've pulled a third of the log up and over the fulcrum.

7 Now put your weight on the end that's up in the air and pivot the far end across the stream, setting it on the other side so that it's stable. See image **c**.

8 Lift the near end of the log off of the fulcrum stones. Move the fulcrum stones out of the way and place the log back in the gap between the foundation stones.

9 Check that the log is stable, and cross it to the other side of the stream.

10 From the far end, pull the log so that it overhangs the stream by about the same amount on both ends.

11 Find two more boulders to use as foundation stones on the far end. Here, the same thing goes as before. Make an indentation for each stone, and keep the gap between them 2 inches less than the width of the log.

12 Rotate the log to take advantage of any protruding stubs that may help keep it stable, and then wedge it between the two foundation stones. Step on the log to make sure that it's stable. See image **d**.

13 Head back across the bridge and make any necessary adjustments to ensure that the other side is still stable. Your bridge is done! See image **e**.

Alternate option #1: Using the methods described above, lay another log of the same length down next to the first, bolster it with stones, and tie the two together using parachute cord. This will make crossing wet logs much easier.

Alternate option #2: If you can't find any downed trees and the stream is less than knee-deep and not moving swiftly, tie your parachute cord to a good-size stick. Throw the stick across the stream into the branches of a tree so that it gets caught in a low branch on the other side. Pull the cord tight and tie it to a branch on your side of the stream. Keep both hands on the cord and cross. You'll get wet, but you'll get across.

MAKE A TEPEE

Tepees rock. They're portable and easy to set up, and they'll keep you dry in the rain, cool in the summer, and warm in the winter. This project shows you how to build an authentic tepee, including an inner liner that helps to vent campfire smoke. This liner also creates an insulating layer of air between the inner and outer canvas, which, in combination with a campfire, gives the tepee its winter warmth. Built with quality materials, it will last for years. See **How Liners Work** illustration on the opposite page.

DIFFICULTY LEVEL:
Backwoodsman

MATERIALS:

60 yards 12-ounce duck canvas, 72-inches wide; mold-, mildew-, and fire-resistant

50 large safety pins

Five 150-yard spools heavy-duty thread in white or natural

Two 50-foot lengths $\frac{3}{8}$-inch twisted, natural-color, polypro rope

Thirty-six $\frac{1}{2}$-inch grommets

Thick catalog or magazine (to use as a hammering base)

20 feet 1-inch nylon tube webbing

100 feet white parachute cord

Five 48-by-$\frac{3}{8}$-inch wooden dowels

50 feet braided $\frac{3}{8}$-inch nylon rope

Seventeen 20-foot-long pine poles whose surfaces have been made smooth

16 tent stakes

3-foot-long thick stick

TOOLS:

Tape measure (50-foot preferable)

Scissors

Sewing machine

5 heavy-duty sewing needles

Piece of colored chalk for marking fabric

Large worktable (4 by 8 feet)

Ballpoint pen

6-foot-long straightedge (A 1x4 board will work well.)

Protractor

Grommet kit for $\frac{1}{2}$-inch grommets (includes hole cutter, punch, and die)

X-ACTO Knife

Heavy engineering or drilling hammer

Lighter

Smoke

Outer Liner

Air

Air

Inner Liner

How Liners Work

INSTRUCTIONS:

A couple of notes before we start: Anytime you cut rope or webbing, heat the ends with the lighter so they won't fray.

When sewing, always reverse over the first inch of the seam. Reverse over the last inch of the seam, as well, and then continue sewing to the edge of the fabric.

1 To start, find a 40- by 20-foot workspace where you'll be able to roll out, pin, and mark up the canvas. Once you've found your spot, sweep it clean of any debris before starting to work.

2 Roll out the canvas and cut two 30-foot-long pieces. Lay the pieces parallel to each other and overlap the edges by 8 inches.

3 Where the two pieces overlap, fold 2 inches of the top piece of fabric in toward the lower piece, so that the raw

edge will be concealed in the overlapping seam. Secure the seam with safety pins every 2 feet along its entire length. See image **a**.

4 Set your machine to zigzag stitch and sew the seam ½ inch from the folded edge, removing the safety pins as you sew, if they're in the way. Now turn the fabric over and do the same thing from the other side, i.e., fold the edge over 2 inches and sew ½ inch from the edge. Both of the raw edges will be concealed inside the seam. See images **b** and **c**. Let's call these "Parallel Seams." See **Parallel Seams** illustration.

5 Roll out and cut a 20-foot piece of canvas. Lay it parallel and centered with the other two pieces. Overlap, fold the edges, pin, and sew both sides as before to form another set of **PARALLEL SEAMS**.

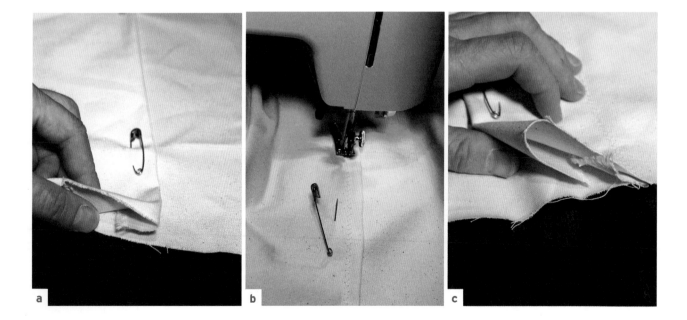

a

b

c

6 Mark the midpoint of the 30-foot side of your canvas with a foot-long chalk line perpendicular to the fabric's edge. I'll refer to the point where the line intersects the edge as the "Center Point."

7 Using the measuring tape and chalk, draw a 15-foot-radius semicircle across the three sections of canvas centered on the **CENTER POINT**. See image **d**.

8 Cut out the semicircle along the chalk line. This canvas semicircle will be the "Tepee Canvas" itself. See **Tepee Canvas** illustration on page 148 and image **e**.

9 With your sewing machine set to zigzag stitch, hem along the straight side of the **TEPEE CANVAS**. Fold the raw edge over 2 inches, pin it, and sew it ½ inch from the folded edge.

10 With the **TEPEE CANVAS'S** chalked **CENTER POINT** side up, lay a 50-foot piece of ⅜-inch twisted polypro rope, centered, along the curved edge of the canvas. Fold the edge over the rope to form a 2-inch hem. Secure with safety pins every 2 feet. There will be about 2½ feet of rope sticking out of each end of the semicircle when you're done. Tie a figure-eight knot into both ends of the rope so that it doesn't get lost inside the hem. See image **f**.

11 Sew the hem as close to the rope as possible and sew over the stitching a second time. This bolt-rope hem will form the bottom of the tepee and needs the extra reinforcement. See image **g**.

12 Reinforce the **PARALLEL SEAMS** as well by sewing another line of stitching ½-inch from each of the previous two. Be sure to sew inside the lines of existing stitches to ensure you'll sew through both layers of fabric. See image **h**.

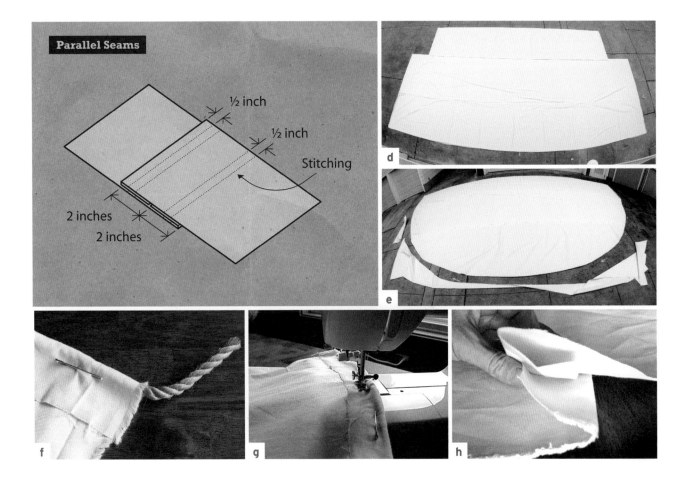

Parallel Seams

½ inch

½ inch

Stitching

2 inches

2 inches

e

f

g

h

13 Now let's make the "Smoke Flaps." Cut out two 6-by-3-foot pieces of canvas and, using a ballpoint pen and a straightedge, lay out a **SMOKE FLAP** on each one according to the illustration. Use a protractor to measure the angles. Be sure to lay the flaps out as mirror images of each other, so you have a left flap and right one. When you cut out the flaps, cut outside the lines by 1 inch. This will give you enough room to sew a hem around each piece. See **Smoke Flap** illustration on page 148.

14 Lay the **SMOKE FLAP** pieces on your worktable. At the corners where the 2½-foot and 5½-foot sides meet, make an X on each flap. These are the "Pocket Corners" that we'll need to reinforce since they'll be under tension from a pair of pine poles. Again, make sure the pockets are the mirror image of each other. At a point 6 inches down from the tip, mark both edges of the **SMOKE FLAP** fabric. Draw a line between the marks. Do this for each flap. For each flap, you'll need three triangular pieces of fabric that are the same size as the corner defined by the line you just drew. Lay these corners over a scrap piece of canvas; trace the size you need and cut out the pieces.

15 Line up one of the three fabric triangles on the back of the **POCKET CORNER** and sew all three sides. Sew the two 6-inch sides again to double up the stitching. See image **i**.

16 Lay the remaining two fabric triangles on top of each other, fold the short sides up to form a 1-inch hem, and sew. This doubled-up fabric triangle is the "Pocket." See image **j**.

17 Lay the **POCKET** seam side up on the front side of the **POCKET CORNER** and sew the two 6-inch sides. Sew these sides twice to double up the stitching. Don't sew the short side! Repeat Steps 13 through 15 for the other **SMOKE FLAP**. Remember: mirror images. See image **k**.

18 Now turn the **POCKETS** inside out. Fold the 1-inch **SMOKE FLAP** hems over toward the **POCKET** side and sew them ½ inch from the edge. See image **l**.

19 Lay the **TEPEE CANVAS** flat with the inside (the seam edges and the **CENTER POINT**) facing up. Using the chalk, draw a 12-by-10-inch isosceles triangle 1 inch from both sides of the **CENTER POINT**. (These triangles will have a 12-inch base and a 10-inch height.) See image **m**. Cut these triangles out 2 inches inside the chalk line and hem the resulting flaps. This will be the spot where the poles exit the top of the tepee. Let's call the notches formed by the missing triangles the "Exit Triangles." See image **n**. For clarification on steps involving the **TEPEE CANVAS** and the **INNER** and **OUTER FLAPS**, refer to the **Tepee Canvas** illustration on page 148.

20 Let's turn our attention back to the **SMOKE FLAP** for a moment. We're now going to attach a grommet to the corner opposite the **POCKET** along the 5½-foot side. The grommet should be placed so that its edges are 1 inch from each side of the corner. Mark the spot.

21 To install the grommet, work on a solid surface. Use a piece of wood or a thick magazine to prevent damage to the surface underneath. Your grommet kit will contain a hole cutter, a cupped anvil and a cylindrical mandrel with a conical tip. Place the hole cutter in the center of your mark. See image **o**. And strike it with a hammer to cut the hole. Trim any frayed canvas away with an X-ACTO knife. See image **p**. Place the coned half of the grommet up through the bottom of the hole and set the grommet in the anvil. (The half of the grommet in the anvil will be the front side when you're done.) See image **q**. Place the other half of the grommet over the cone, sandwiching the canvas between the two halves. Place the pointed end of the mandrel into the cone and strike the top of it sharply with the hammer. See image **r** and **s**. The cone will deform down and the grommet will be complete.

22 Now we're going to sew the **SMOKE FLAPS** onto the straight edge of the **TEPEE CANVAS**. Here's how. Position the flaps so that the **POCKETS** are face down, toward the centerline of the **TEPEE CANVAS** but facing away from the **CENTER POINT**. On both flaps, the **TOP**

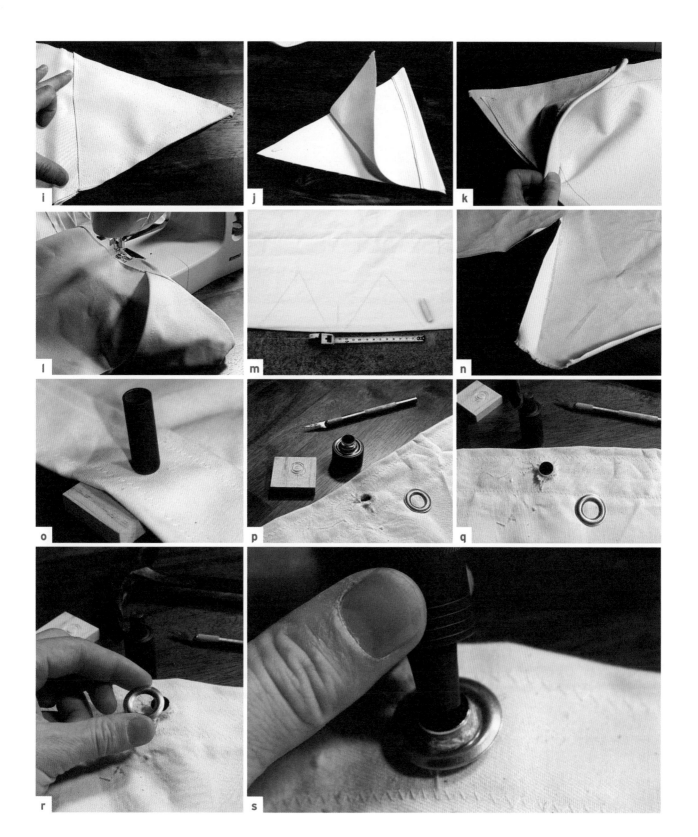

MAKE A TEPEE   147

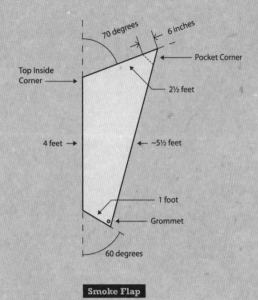

70 degrees

6 inches

Pocket Corner

Top Inside Corner

2½ feet

4 feet

~5½ feet

1 foot

Grommet

60 degrees

Smoke Flap

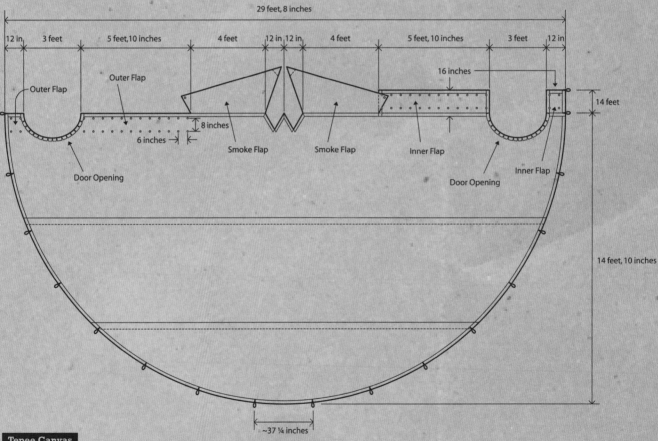

29 feet, 8 inches

12 in | 3 feet | 5 feet, 10 inches | 4 feet | 12 in | 12 in | 4 feet | 5 feet, 10 inches | 3 feet | 12 in

16 inches

14 feet

Outer Flap

Outer Flap

Inner Flap

8 inches

6 inches

Door Opening

Smoke Flap

Smoke Flap

Inner Flap

Door Opening

Inner Flap

14 feet, 10 inches

~37 ¼ inches

Tepee Canvas

INSIDE corner should just touch the outside corner of the **EXIT TRIANGLES** you cut in Step 19. Overlap the **TEPEE CANVAS** and the **SMOKE FLAPS** by 2 inches, and double-check that the outside of the **TEPEE CANVAS** and **POCKETS** on the **SMOKE FLAPS** are both face-down. Safety-pin the flaps in place, then sew them to the **TEPEE CANVAS** using two rows of stitching, the first ¼ inch from the edge of the flap, the second 1 inch from the edge. See **Tepee Canvas** illustration.

23 Now let's reinforce the area where poles exit. Cut a piece of canvas measuring 3 feet by 18 inches. Lay it centered on the centerline of the **TEPEE CANVAS**, over the **EXIT TRIANGLES** and overlapping the **SMOKE FLAPS** by 3 inches.

24 Safety-pin the four corners. Feel the edges of the **EXIT TRIANGLES** underneath, and mark them with a piece of chalk. Now cut another set of exit triangles out of this reinforcement canvas—however, make them about ¼ inch bigger than the ones in the **TEPEE CANVAS**. Sew along the outer edge of this canvas piece. Do it twice to form a double row of stitches. See images **t** and **u**.

25 Great! Now let's work on the "Inner Flap." This will be composed of two pieces of canvas sewn to one half of

the **TEPEE CANVAS'S** straight edge. They'll form the connection to the other half of the straight edge when the tepee is set up. This connection is made by a double row of grommets pinned together with wooden dowels. Start by cutting two pieces of canvas, one 20 by 74 inches and another 20 by 16 inches. Fold all of the raw edges over 2 inches to form a hem and sew them 1 inch from the folded edge. Do this for both pieces.

26 Make sure the **TEPEE CANVAS** is still lying "inside up" and place the larger piece, lengthwise, hemmed side up, against the straight edge of the **TEPEE CANVAS**, just below where the **SMOKE FLAP** is attached. Looking down at the **TEPEE CANVAS** with the curved edge at the bottom, I attached this piece along the edge to the right of the **CENTER POINT**. Overlap the edges of the two pieces of canvas by 2 inches and sew ½ inch from the edge. Sew again 1½ inches from the edge. Let's call the left half of the **TEPEE CANVAS'S** straight edge the "Outer Flap." See **Tepee Canvas** illustration.

27 Where the **INNER FLAP** and the **SMOKE FLAP** meet, reinforce the two corners with a double layer of 3-by-6-inch canvas. Sew around all of the edges. See image **v**.

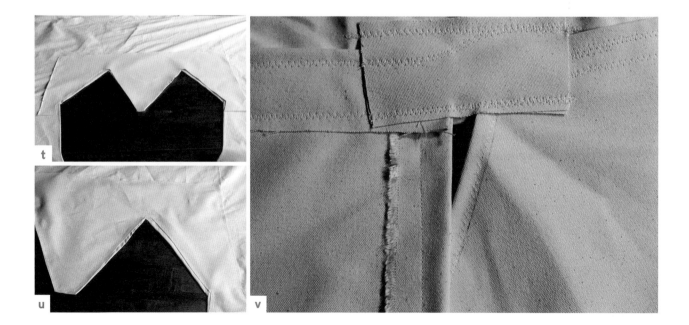

w

x

28 Do the same with the smaller piece. Orient it hem-side up, with its short side along the same half of the **TEPEE CANVAS'S** straight edge. Attach it so that its bottom edge touches the outer, curved edge of the **TEPEE CANVAS**—or get it as close as you can. Overlap 2 inches onto the **TEPEE CANVAS'S** straight edge and sew as before. The gap between these two pieces of fabric will form the door. See image **w**.

29 Let's work on the door now. Fold both corners of the **TEPEE CANVAS** down to the middle of the curved side. The canvas will now be a quarter-circle shape, and the two halves of the straight edge will lie parallel to each other. The **INNER FLAP** will overlap about 16 inches.

30 Now draw a chalk oval on the canvas to represent the door. The oval should measure 3 feet high by 2½ feet wide. It should be centered horizontally on the seam of the **OUTER FLAP** and vertically over the gap between the two parts of the **INNER FLAP**. Mark the canvas on both the **INNER** and **OUTER FLAPS**. See **Chalk Line for Door** illustration.

31 Using your scissors, cut 2 inches within the chalk line to form the door. Again, do this—and the next couple of steps—on both sides.

32 Cut into the edge of the door perpendicularly to the chalk line. Do this every 3 inches all around the edge to form a series of tabs. See image **x**.

33 Fold the tabs to the inside (to match the seams on the other hems), ½ inch past the chalk line, and attach each one with a safety pin. Then sew them down both ½ inch and 1½ inches from the door's edge.

34 Cut the nylon webbing into seventeen 10-inch strips. Melt all of the cut edges with the lighter to prevent them from unraveling.

35 Now make loops out of the webbing. To form the loop, fold the webbing in half, giving one side a half twist just before putting the ends together. Space 16 of the loops evenly around the semicircular edge of the **TEPEE CANVAS**. (They'll be spaced about 37¼ inches apart.)

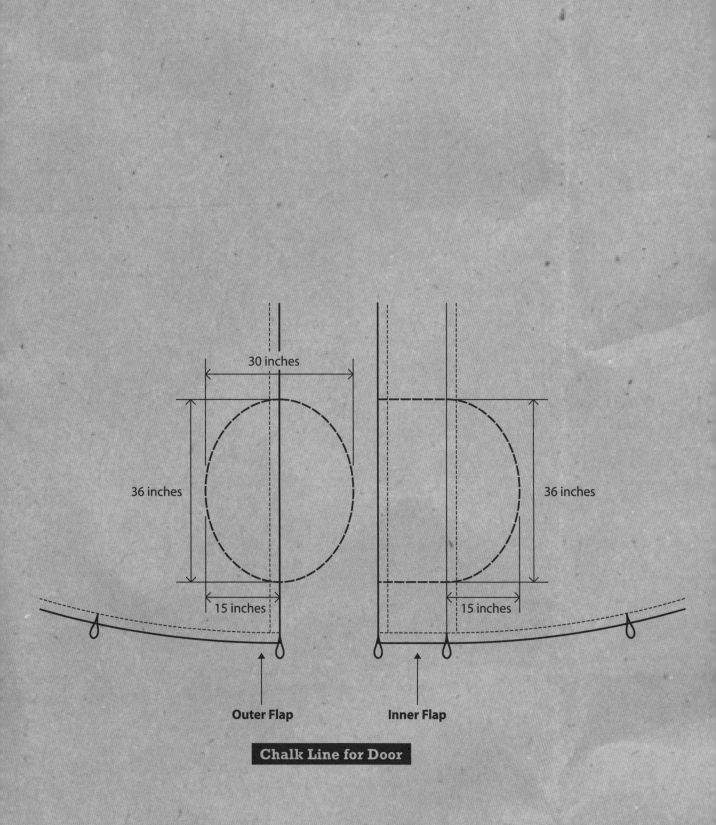

30 inches

36 inches

15 inches

Outer Flap

36 inches

15 inches

Inner Flap

Chalk Line for Door

Save the last loop for the corner of the **INNER FLAP**. (See **Tepee Canvas** illustration on page 148.) Lay the end of the loop so that it just overlaps the hem and sew it down with an X-and-box pattern, like this: Between the hem's raw edge and the bolt rope, sew back and forth across the webbing. Do this in two places, about 1 inch apart. Between these two stitches sew an X, going over it twice, as well. In the photo you'll see that I've sewed a Z so far. See image **y**.

36 Now let's add the grommets. The grommets, and some dowels, will later fasten the left and right halves of the straight edge together. On the **TEPEE CANVAS'S OUTER FLAP** mark an X with the ballpoint pen that's 4 inches above the bottom edge of the tepee (the edge with the sewn-in rope) and 3 inches from the straight edge. This is where the first grommet goes.

37 Make another mark 8 inches to the left of the first. That's where the second grommet goes. The grommets will march up the front of the tepee in groups of two.

38 Make another set of marks 6 inches above each of the two just made. Now you should have four marks below the doorway.

39 Make marks for another set of grommets above the top of the door. The right-hand grommet should be centered 2 inches above the highest point of the door opening and 3 inches from the straight edge of the canvas. Center the left-hand grommet 8 inches to the left of the right-hand one.

40 Continue making marks in groups of two, every 6 inches up to where the **SMOKE FLAP** attaches to the straight edge. See image **z**.

41 Using the hole cutter, cut out all of the grommet holes on this half of the flap.

42 Again, arrange the **TEPEE CANVAS** into a quarter-circle as in Step 29, making sure that the **INNER FLAP** is underneath the grommet holes you just cut. Make sure the seams and the door line up perfectly, transfer the hole positions to the **INNER FLAP**, and cut them out as before.

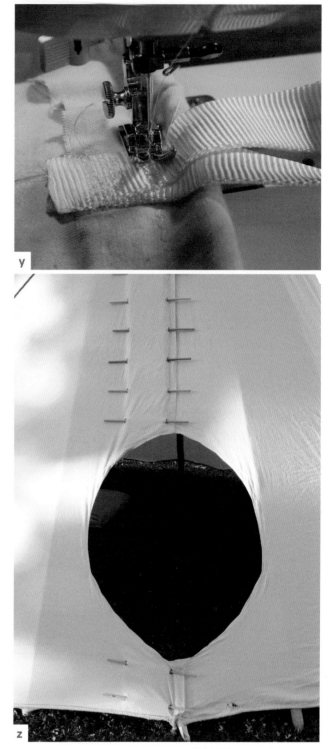

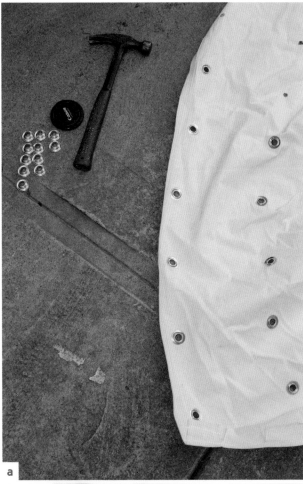

a

b

43 Turn the **TEPEE CANVAS** so that the inside is facing up and affix a grommet to each of the holes on both halves of the flap. Remember that the side of the grommet facing down while you work will be the front side when you're done. See image **a**.

44 Add two grommets to the triangular flap at the **CENTER POINT** of the canvas as well. Locate them 1 inch from the edges and 3 inches from the flap's tip. See image **b**.

45 Attach a 15-foot piece of polypro rope to each **SMOKE FLAP** grommet using a bowline. OK—the **TEPEE CANVAS** is done!

46 OK—let's work on the "Inner Liner." This will be the tepee's inner wall. To start, roll out two 41-foot-by-10-inch lengths of canvas. The goal is to make 30 trapezoidal pieces of canvas measuring 26 inches at the top and 40 inches at the bottom. See **Inner Liner Sections** illustration on page 154 for the best way to lay out the pieces.

47 Now sew the 38 liner pieces together. To do this, double up the canvas pieces and lay them into a fifteen-section arc, two pieces thick. All of the 26-inch sides should link to form the inside part of the arc, and the 40-inch sides link to form the outside part of the arc. Make sure the long sides of the canvas sections overlap each other by two inches and pin them together.

48 Fold the two 26-inch sides at the top of each section inward 1 inch and sew ½ inch from the edge. Do the same for the 40-inch sides and the long edges and the beginning and end of the arc. Lastly, sew the long, overlapping edges of each section ½ inch from each sides of the 2-inch overlap. That means where the sections meet, there will be two rows of stitching 1 inch apart. These double-wall baffles that form the **INNER LINER** will provide a nice insulating layer to the outside.

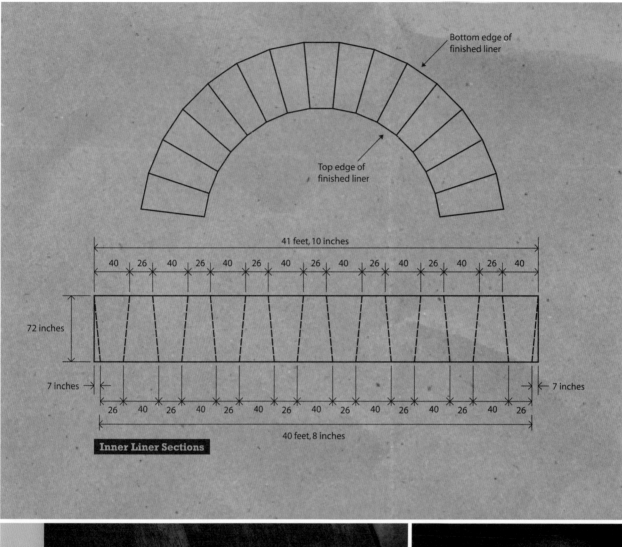

Bottom edge of finished liner

Top edge of finished liner

41 feet, 10 inches

40 | 26 | 40 | 26 | 40 | 26 | 40 | 26 | 40 | 26 | 40 | 26 | 40 | 26 | 40

72 inches

7 inches →|← |← 7 inches

26 | 40 | 26 | 40 | 26 | 40 | 26 | 40 | 26 | 40 | 26 | 40 | 26 | 40 | 26

40 feet, 8 inches

Inner Liner Sections

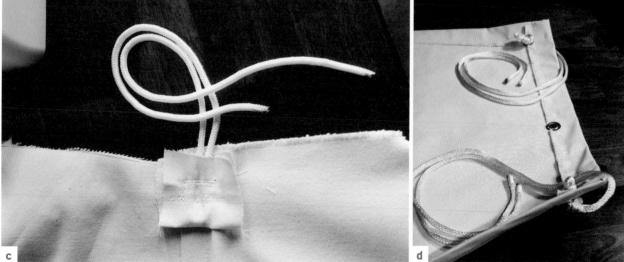

c

d

49 Cut 32 pieces of 24-inch-long para cord and heat the ends with the lighter so they won't unravel.

50 Cut 32 pieces of 4-by-2-inch canvas. These lengths of cord and canvas will form the "Ties" that hold the **INNER LINER** in place.

51 Fold a length of para cord in half, then fold a small piece of canvas over the bight at the midpoint. Place these on the top edge of the **INNER LINER** at the seams where each of the 26-inch sides meet. The cord should be oriented so it hangs up over the edge of the canvas, not down onto it. Stitch back and forth over the canvas square and para cord five or six times, moving the material sideways as you go. See image **c**.

52 Sew another **TIE** onto the seam 6 inches from the lower edge, this time with the cord ends hanging down. Do this for each seam as well as both short sides of the liner. Attaching the **TIES** 6 inches from the bottom allows the lower edge of the liner to skirt the ground.

53 Cut the wooden dowels into 12-inch-long pieces.

54 Now let's make the "Door Flap." Start by cutting two pieces of fabric that measure 38 by 60 inches.

55 With your pen, lay out the shape of the finished piece in the middle of one of the pieces of fabric according to the **Door Flap** illustration. Lay the pieces on top of each other, pin them, and cut them out 2 inches outside of what will be the finished edge. Fold the edges in 2 inches. Check that the door will be 30 inches wide at its vertical midpoint. Sew around the perimeter ½ inch, and 1½ inches from the folded edge. With a midpoint width of 30 inches, the **DOOR FLAP** will fit perfectly snugly in the door of the tepee. Install two grommets along the top of the door, one in each corner, centered 2 inches from the finished edges. Adding one in the middle is optional. See image **d**.

56 Cut two pieces of 24-inch nylon webbing and heat the ends as before so they won't unravel. Fold the pieces in half and arrange them so that they overlap the left edge

of the door (the right edge when seen from the outside of the door) by 2 inches. Position one at the widest point and one at the midpoint. For each piece of webbing, make sure that one end overlaps the front side of the door, and one overlaps the back side. Sew the ends of the webbing to the door with an X pattern as in Step 35. Each piece of webbing now forms a loop. Cut each loop at its midpoint and heat the ends. These will later be part of the door handle.

57 Sew a 24-inch para cord **TIE** to the lower right corner (as seen from the inside) of the door using the previous method. This **TIE** will form a pivot point for the door.

58 Fold two 4-foot pieces of ⅜-inch nylon rope in half and tie an overhand knot into the bights. Thread the two loose ends of each piece through the grommets in the corners of the door flaps. Pass them through from back to front. Tie another overhand knot in the ropes on the front side of the door. Tie these ropes to the pine poles, when the tepee is set up, to hold the door in place. See image **e** on page 156.

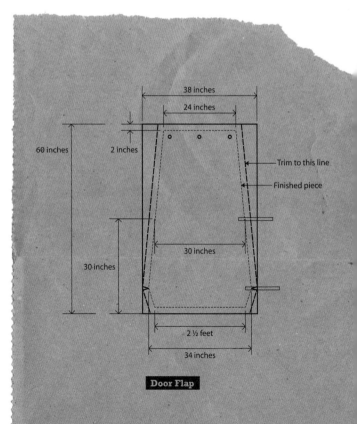

Door Flap

e

f

g

h

59 Let's set it up! Cut a 25-foot length of ⅜-inch nylon rope. Tie a bowline in the end to form a loop. Select the three thickest poles and wrap the loop around them, 4 feet from the tops. Pull a bight through the loop and tie it off on the standing part of the rope. This will be the "Main Rope." See image **f**.

60 Set the poles up to form a tripod. Place one of the poles a little farther from the other two (to form an oblong circle). This will be your "Primary Pole." Ensure that the PRIMARY POLE is facing downwind. See the **Pole and Sleeping Bag Arrangement** illustration and image **g**.

61 Evenly place four poles between each of the three legs of the tripod to complete the oblong circle. See image **h**.

62 Lay out your TEPEE CANVAS so the inside is facing up. Measure the gap between the two grommets near the CENTER POINT of the canvas. Take a 3-foot piece of

nylon rope and tie two figure-eight knots at the midpoint about as far apart as the gap between the grommets. Thread the ends of the rope up through the grommets from underneath. Remove the pole to the right of the PRIMARY POLE and lay it onto the CENTER POINT. The top of the pole should be about 4 feet from the CENTER POINT. Wrap the rope around the pole as many times as you can and tie the ends with a square knot. See image **i**.

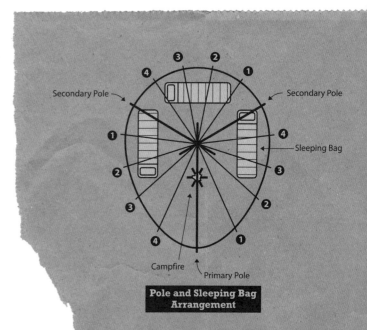

Secondary Pole

Secondary Pole

Sleeping Bag

Campfire

Primary Pole

Pole and Sleeping Bag Arrangement

63 Pull the **MAIN ROPE** tight. Walk around the structure until you've put about four wraps in the rope. Tie the rope off on the **PRIMARY POLE**.

64 Take the pole with the attached **TEPEE CANVAS** and put it back in place. Take a wrap around it with the **MAIN ROPE** and tie the rope off at the **PRIMARY POLE** with a round turn and two half hitches. If you're a little shy of rope, a clove hitch will do.

65 Now slowly unwrap the canvas and drape it over the poles until you can match up the **INNER FLAP** and **OUTER FLAP** grommets at the **PRIMARY POLE**.

66 Insert the 12-inch dowels through the grommets to knit the front of the tepee together. See image **j**.

67 Go into the tepee and push all of the poles outward as much as you can until the canvas is stretched tight. Make sure to leave a 4-inch gap between the ground and the tepee's bottom edge.

68 Slip the tent stakes through the webbing loops along the lower edge and hammer them into the ground. Make sure you don't reduce the gap at the bottom edge of the tepee to anything less than 2 inches. Three inches is ideal.

69 Place the tips of the two remaining pine poles into the **POCKETS** on the **SMOKE FLAPS** and walk the other ends around to the back of the tepee. The poles should cross, so that the pole holding open the left-hand flap is behind the tepee on the right, and vice versa. See image **k** on page 156.

70 Tie each **SMOKE FLAP** rope to a tent stake, pull the stakes down and away from the tepee, and hammer them into the ground. These ropes should not cross.

71 Tie a 50-foot piece of nylon rope to the **PRIMARY POLE** about 5 feet from the lower end. Move one pole to the right (as seen from inside the tepee) and wrap around the pole. Keep doing this all around the tepee until you get back to the **PRIMARY POLE**. Tie the rope off. This is your "Interior Rope." See image **l** on page 158.

k

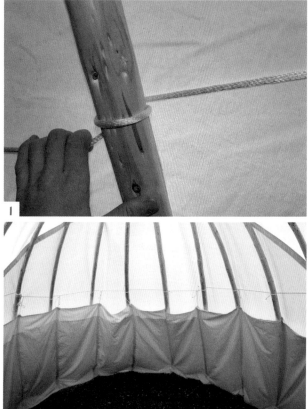

l

m

72 Starting at the **PRIMARY POLE**, tie the **INNER LINER** to the **INTERIOR ROPE**, making sure the clean-looking seams are facing the interior of the tepee. Tie the lower edge of the liner to the bottoms of the poles and lay the 6 inches of extra fabric toward the interior. See image **m**.

73 Tie the top of the **DOOR FLAP** to the poles so that the bottom almost touches the ground. When the door is properly closed, though, the bottom half will hang outside the tepee even though the top half is tied on the inside. Tie a thick 3-foot-long stick to the webbing on the side of the door and tie the cord in the lower corner to a pole outside. The stick will act as a door handle, and its weight will keep the door closed.

74 Dig a hole in the middle of the tepee 18 inches wide by 6 inches deep and line it with stones 2 to 4 inches thick. Spread the dirt outside and build a fire in your new stone-lined hearth.

RESOURCES

BIODEGRADABLE LATRINE

www.bagtonature.com

www.biobagusa.com

www.felinepine.com

CAMP GEAR

www.amazon.com

www.coleman.com

www.ems.com

www.homedepot.com

www.lowes.com

www.nps.gov

www.rei.com

www.thecompassstore.com

www.walmart.com

DISC GOLF

www.discgolfcenter.com

www.discnation.com

www.everythingdiscgolf.com

EDIBLE PLANTS AND BUGS

www.groedibles.com

www.safetycentral.com

www.survivaltopics.com

www.wilderness-survival.net

The Complete Guide to Edible Wild Plants by U.S. Dept. of the Army

Identifying and Harvesting Edible and Medicinal Plants in Wild (and Not So Wild) Places by Steve Brill and Evelyn Dean

GEOCACHING

www.geocaching.com

www.groundspeak.com

www.joyofgeocaching.com

www.navicache.com

www.opencaching.com

The Complete Idiot's Guide to Geocaching by Jack W. Peters

The Essential Guide to Geocaching by Mike Dyer

PANNING FOR GOLD

www.blackcatmining.com

www.goldfeverprospecting.com

PORTABLE PVC FISHING GEAR

www.ffo-tackle.com

www.parachute-cord.com

www.woofish.com

SLACKLINING

www.balancecommunity.com

www.gibbonslacklines.com

www.landcruising-slacklines.de

www.rocknrescue.com

www.slackline.com

SOLAR SHOWER

www.findtape.com

www.freckleface.com

www.pleasanthillgrain.com

SURVIVAL KIT

www.survivalkitfood.com

www.survivalkitsonline.com

www.thereadystore.com

www.thinkgeek.com

TARP SURFING

www.tarps.com

www.tarpsplus.com

TEPEE

www.rosebrand.com

www.tipi.com

TORCH

www.dube.com

www.onlinemetals.com

WAR BONNET

www.crazycrow.com

www.homesew.com

www.joann.com

www.ostrich.com

INDEX